Jane Smiley's
A Thousand Acres

CONTINUUM CONTEMPORARIES

Also available in this series

Forthcoming in this series

· **JANE SMILEY'S**

A

Thousand

Acres

A READER'S GUIDE

SUSAN FARRELL

CONTINUUM | NEW YORK | LONDON

2001

The Continuum International Publishing Group Inc
370 Lexington Avenue, New York, NY 10017

The Continuum International Publishing Group Ltd
The Tower Building, 11 York Road, London SE1 7NX

Printed in the United States of America

Library of Congress Cataloging-in-Publication Data

Farrell, Susan Elizabeth, 1963–
    Jane Smiley's A thousand acres : a reader's guide / Susan Farrell.
        p. cm.— (Continuum contemporaries)
    Includes bibliographical references and index.
    ISBN 0-8264-5235-3 (pbk. alk. paper)
    1. Smiley, Jane. Thousand acres. 2. Inheritance and succession in
literature. 3. Fathers and daughters in literature. 4. Lear, King
(Legendary character) 5. Rural families in literature. 6. Farm life in
literature. 7. Iowa—In literature. I. Title. II. Series.
    PS3569.M39 T47 2001
    813'.54—dc21

                                    2001028962

Contents

The Novelist

FAMILY ORIGINS

Jane Smiley's parents met in Paris in 1945. Her mother, Frances Graves (born 1921), from Wood River, Illinois, was a member of the Women's Army Corps and working in Paris as an army correspondent. Smiley's father, James Laverne Smiley (born 1915), had moved from his home in Kalamazoo, Michigan, to attend the U.S. Military Academy at West Point. After graduating, he served in World War II and was stationed in France at the end of the war. Although they first met in Europe, it wasn't until several years later that the couple renewed their relationship and married. In 1946, Frances took a job as a reporter for a Memphis, Tennessee newspaper. James went to Los Angeles where he worked as an aeronautical engineer at Hughes Aircraft. In 1948, James contacted Frances by letter which led to a correspondence and resparked their interest in one another. Frances moved to Los Angeles where she and James were married on December 7 of that year. Their first (and only) child, Jane Graves Smiley, was born in Los Angeles, California, on September 26, 1949.

The marriage of Frances and James was troubled from the beginning. Soon after Jane's birth, James was treated for mental problems possibly related to his service in the war. The couple divorced when Jane was four years old. Her mother brought Jane to St. Louis where Frances could be close to her family and resume her career as a journalist. While Frances worked for various local newspapers, Jane spent the days with her mother's parents and grew up surrounded by aunts, uncles, and cousins to whom she remained very close even as an adult. The complexities and subtleties of family interaction, which she was able to observe as a child growing up in a large extended family in the Midwest, came to be a dominant theme in Smiley's adult fiction. In fact, she writes that:

The first novel I ever knew was our family. We had every necessary element, from the wealth of incident both domestic (my grandfather wearing his bowling shirt to my aunt's wedding because nothing else was ironed) and historical (my uncle in World War II, lying in the belly of a bomber, photographing successful destruction), to the large cast of characters — my mother and her four siblings, their husbands and wives, and many cousins, the thirteen children who made up our generation. . . . Our novel had as many voices as it had characters, each eagerly contributing his or her own detail, his or her version. Our novel had a ready audience — us grandchildren; we asked for the stories, looked at the pictures, delved into the deep background. (Smiley, "Afterword," 1996, 241)

Smiley's maternal grandparents, whom she describes as the "beginning" of her family's novel, were especially influential in her life. She remembers her grandfather, David Berger Graves, as a dashing, forceful, and strict man, the "patriarch" she knew best. While he demanded respect and obedience from his family, his hot temper and sternness were mitigated by what Smiley remembers as a "terrific sense of humor" (Smiley "Imposing," 1992, 28). Smiley describes her grandmother, Ethel Ingeborg Doolittle, as having the "special gift of cherishing [each of the cousins] individually" (Smiley, "Afterword," 1996, 241). She was a practical, energetic woman who learned lessons of survival from her own mother, who had emigrated to the United States from Norway at the age of sixteen. A new set of step-relations was added to the mix of grandparents, cousins, and aunts when Smiley's mother married William J. Nuelle in 1960. Not only did Nuelle have custody of two adopted children, Susan and William, from a previous marriage, but he and Frances later had two children of their own, David and Frances, Jane's half-brother and sister.

As a child, Smiley enjoyed English and history at school, but had a passion for horses. "I was obsessed with horses my whole childhood," Smiley says. "That was my first and maybe ultimately my strongest obsession in some ways" (Ross, 1990, 411). She first rode a horse when she was four years old and had two horses of her own while growing up. After graduating from high school, she worked for the summer as a horse groom in a camp in Virginia. Smiley's love of horses fits alongside her fascination with family interchange as a recurring preoccupation in her later fiction. Her first work of fiction, *Barn Blind*, as well as her tenth, *Horse Heaven*, focus especially on the ins and outs of lives dedicated to breeding, showing, and racing horses. While abandoning her childhood obsession for most of her adult life, Smiley's success as a novelist has allowed her to indulge her girlhood fantasies. She currently lives in the Carmel Valley in Northern California, where she breeds and raises thoroughbred race horses.

EDUCATION

Smiley's path to becoming a successful author included a solid education. She speaks of herself as being part of the first generation of girls foretold by Virginia Woolf in *A Room of One's Own*, a generation "for whom education was so normal that we took our career choices for granted" (Smiley, "Shakespeare," 1999, 163). Smiley recalls that everyone—her parents, her professors, her boyfriend, herself—took her education seriously, never assuming that her goal should be to get married and have children, but rather to work. And the work that Smiley planned to do was the work of a novelist. "My career plan was straightforward," she says, "to read as many books as possible and to get as much praise for my own writing as possible" (Smiley, "Shakespeare," 1999, 163). These plans were first formulated in high school and even junior high, where, Smiley remembers, she was influenced by three books that she credits with shaping her future writing. Two of these were novels: *Giants in the Earth* by O. E. Rölvaag, which she read in eighth grade and *David Copperfield* by Charles Dickens, which she read in ninth grade. What impressed her about Rölvaag's novel were the hardships endured by Per Hansa and his family, the realistic terror with which Rölvaag depicted the experience of western settlement. What she loved about Dickens was his style. *David Copperfield*, she says, taught her how potentially complex and lively a form the novel could be. The other book which Smiley remembers as an influence was a science book, *The Web of Life*, which introduced her to ecology and taught her to appreciate the connectedness of people to the earth. Smiley's early ecological awareness blossoms into her later questioning of the dangers inherent in traditional farming evident in *A Thousand Acres*, a novel which also stresses connections between people and the earth as Smiley explicitly links the exploitation of women to the exploitation of the land itself.

At Vassar College, where she enrolled in the fall of 1967, Smiley took courses in English literature ranging from Old English to the beginning of the twentieth century. She liked long complex novels like *Pamela, Emma, Tom Jones*, the works of Tolstoy, and of George

Eliot. She was particularly fond of her Shakespeare professor, Harriett Hawkins, whom Smiley describes as a compelling, supportive teacher. Smiley had read a Shakespeare play each year beginning in seventh grade (including *King Lear*), but it wasn't until college that she says she read *Lear* with real seriousness. It was in Professor Hawkins' class that Smiley first noticed that her reaction to the play did not conform to the standard interpretations. Smiley has grappled with her relationship to Shakespeare in all of her writing, but most significantly in *A Thousand Acres*, her retelling of the Lear saga. While she believes that "every writer of English has a relationship to [Shakespeare]" and that "English cannot be written without Shakespeare, or, for that matter, read without Shakespeare," she wasn't willing to go so far as a later office mate who "seriously considered Shakespeare to be an incarnation of the deity" (Smiley, "Shakespeare," 1999, 165). Rather, she saw Shakespeare as a writer to model herself after, someone who was "adept at comedy and tragedy and irony and characterization and poetry and prose, a person of wide-ranging interests and skillful at the illusion of expertise, lively and sober by turns, familiar with the full range of emotions, able to believably extrapolate from the quotidian life of a citizen to the epic life of a king or a queen" (Smiley, "Shakespeare," 1999, 165) Nevertheless, Smiley notes that drama was not going to be her chosen form. "I grew up in a family of story-tellers, gossipers, natural narrators," she recounts, "We did not mimic voices or take parts or perform. We specialized in irony of tone" (Smiley, "Shakespeare," 1999, 162). It wasn't until later, in graduate school, when she encountered old Icelandic sagas that she truly felt she had found the particular voice of her own family.

While an undergraduate at Vassar, Smiley met and began to date a young Yale student, John Whiston, who was something of a student activist. She remembers long, complex, political discussions between herself and Whiston as students: "The only things my boyfriend and I talked about were class warfare, racism, endangered species . . . Marxist analysis" (Smiley, "Shakespeare," 1999, 164). The couple experimented with the radical, hippie lifestyle of the era when they lived together in a leftist commune in New Haven, Connecticut during the summer of 1970. They married a few months later, on September 4, 1970. Although, according to Smiley, politics had not been a special interest of hers before going to Vassar, she reports that her relationship with Whiston "changed and shaped [her] sense of the world from top to bottom," that however "juvenile" or "half-baked" their talks might have been, they instilled in her a political consciousness and made her ripe for the feminist ideas which would later "flow into it" (Smiley, "Shakespeare," 1999, 164). Certainly, *A Thousand Acres* arises not only from Smiley's academic encounters with Shakespeare and the great realistic novelists, but from her political awakening and early feminist impulses as well.

After graduating from Vassar College in 1971 with a B.A. and a major in English, Smiley moved with Whiston to Iowa, where he enrolled as a graduate student in medieval history at the University of Iowa. Because she had not been accepted into the prestigious Iowa Writer's Workshop as she had hoped, Smiley lived the life of a graduate student wife. She recounts working at one point making teddy bears in a factory in order to make ends meet. Through her husband, though, she soon met a professor of Old Norse and began auditing his class where she first began to read the Icelandic sagas. She says that because she was not a good student of Old Norse, she had to read and translate very slowly. But perhaps because her consumption of them was so slow and painstaking, the sagas left permanent images in her mind. Her 1988 book, *The Greenlanders*, is a long, historical novel set in fourteenth-century Greenland and based on the sagas that so influenced her.

In December of 1972, Smiley was accepted into the Ph.D. program in English at the University of Iowa. Her decision to pursue the Ph.D. was not a repudiation of her ambitions as a creative writer. Just before completing the work required for her master's degree, she was finally accepted into the Iowa Writer's Workshop, a program she began in the fall of 1974. In 1975, Smiley received her Master of Arts Degree in English while also taking classes at the Writer's Workshop. Her marriage with Whiston dissolved that same year. The couple was divorced in November of 1975. The next year, 1976, Smiley received her Master of Fine Arts Degree from the Iowa Writer's Workshop. Still working toward her Ph.D., she accepted a Fulbright Fellowship during the 1976–1977 academic year that gave her the opportunity to travel to Iceland, where she planned to conduct research toward her proposed dissertation on the Icelandic sagas. "In Iceland," Smiley remembers, "I exchanged the sociable, coupled, communal life I had lived in Iowa City for a solitary one, my many companions and amusements for reading, reading, and only reading" (Smiley, "Shakespeare," 1999, 167). Some of the books Smiley recalls being influenced by during this period of solitude and reflection in her life include *Anna Karenina* and *War and Peace, Madame Bovary, The Brothers Karamazov, The Grapes of Wrath*, and every Icelandic saga which had been translated into English. Smiley was also able to focus on her own writing during this period, producing several short stories and conceiving the main ideas and plots of her first two novels as well as of *The Greenlanders*. Upon her return from Iceland, Smiley ended up submitting a creative dissertation, a collection of short stories titled *Harmes and Feares*, rather than the scholarly research she had planned. The dissertation was accepted and Smiley received her Ph.D. in medieval literature from the University of Iowa in 1978. That same year, she married William Silag, a historian with whom she eventually had two daughters, Phoebe Graves Silag and Lucy Gallagher Silag.

EARLY WRITING CAREER

Smiley held several temporary academic appointments until 1981 when she settled into a full time position at Iowa State University in Ames, Iowa, where she taught literature and creative writing until 1997. Smiley's first three novels appeared in quick succession in the early 1980's. *Barn Blind,* her first novel, was published by Harper and Row in 1980. It tells the story of a horse raising family in Iowa whose four children are dominated by their single-minded mother, Kate Karlson. Kate's determination that at least one of her children will become a member of the U.S. Olympic Equestrian Team causes in her a blindness to her children's individuality and ultimately leads to a family tragedy. The novel was well received critically. Many reviewers praised it as an extremely accomplished first novel, particularly in its character development and realistic depiction of adolescent confusion. Smiley's second novel, *At Paradise Gate,* appeared in 1981. Drawing heavily on Smiley's own family background, *At Paradise Gate* depicts the gathering together of 77-year-old Ike Robison's wife, three daughters, and granddaughter during his last few days of life. The three generations of women argue, reminisce, and care for Ike as he lies dying. Although accused of being "belabored" and overly "talky" in places (Untitled *Kirkus Review,* 1981), the novel was also praised for its remarkable and moving depiction of family closeness and bitterness, and for its richness of emotional detail. Smiley surprised many readers with the 1984 publication of *Duplicate Keys,* her third novel which seems to abandon her previous concerns with the generational conflict of large Iowa families. Set in New York City, *Duplicate Keys* is a murder mystery revolving around a group of friends with ties to members of a failed rock n-roll band. When two of the band members are found murdered in an apartment that all the friends had keys to, suspicions and fears begin to arise. Many reviewers note, however, that the mystery itself is incidental to Smiley's more important themes in the book—her portrayal of friendship, love, and betrayal, of change and growing older. Perhaps *Duplicate Keys*, then, is not such a departure from her earlier work as it may seem at first. Though she dropped the at times painful, at times joyous relationships between blood relatives, Smiley depicts the same relations worked out in a forged family, a group of friends who have known each other for years, moved from city to city together, and created their own family network.

Smiley describes the fourteen months from May 1984 to July 1985, when *Duplicate Keys* had been finished and she was writing her next two works, *The Greenlanders* and a collection of short fiction, *The Age of Grief*, as the "most important period of [her] life as a writer" (Smiley, "Shakespeare," 1999, 167). In June of 1984, she traveled to England, Denmark, and Greenland on a research trip. She remembers that before she left Iowa, she had "68 awkward pages" of manuscript for *The Greenlanders* written. But the nascent novel didn't take hold of her until after her return, when it consumed her attention more than any of her previous novels. Although she had many distractions by this time—two children, a house, and a husband of six years—she describes herself as "frantic with inspiration" for her new novel. While her usual routine involved writing for only a few hours each day, by the time she finished *The Greenlanders* in the summer of 1985 she was writing all day and had over 1100 pages of manuscript. "I was 35 years old and dissatisfied with my marriage," Smiley explains, adding that she was also convinced that *The Greenlanders* was her masterwork and that "the process [she] was going through was a necessary process for such a work," though she admits she didn't like what this obsession had done to her life, to her routine, and to her sense of self (Smiley, "Shakespeare," 1999, 168). Following the completion of her Icelandic epic, Smiley very quickly wrote the novella which became the first story in her collection, *The Age of Grief*. Perhaps something of a catharsis for Smiley, the story is told from the perspective of a 35 year old dentist with three daughters who must come to terms with his crumbling marriage and the disappointments of his family life. Smiley's own marriage to William Silag ended in divorce in February of 1986. She would later, in July of 1987, marry Stephen Mortensen, a screenwriter with whom she had one son, Axel James.

Published in 1987, *The Age of Grief* met glowing reviews, especially for its title story. One reviewer described the story as "a lovely and very sad meditation on the evanescence and durability of love" while another labeled it "infinitely satisfying" and "a glorious achievement for Jane Smiley" (Kakutani, 1987, C21; Bernays, 1987, 12). *The Greenlanders* (588 pages in its final printed form) came out a year later. Although it was read by a much smaller audience than the story collection, something Smiley expected and was not unhappy about, it too was very well received; reviewers praised its beauty, austerity, and historical accuracy. Both books were translated from English, increasing Smiley's readership and beginning to make her internationally known. Perhaps enouraged by the reaction to *The Age of Grief*, Smiley's next project was a return to the form of the novella. *Ordinary Love and Goodwill*, two short novels "of equally extraordinary power and perception," according to reviewer and novelist Josephine Humphreys, were published together in book form in 1989. But it was the publication of *A Thousand Acres* in 1991 that cemented Smiley's literary reputation.

SUCCESS AS A WRITER

Smiley recounts several small, fortuitous accidents which led to the
genesis of *A Thousand Acres*. First, she describes sitting at a Mc-
Donald's restaurant in Delhi, New York, in the summer of 1987,
briefly and offhandedly telling her husband, Stephen Mortensen,
about her idea for rewriting *King Lear*. This particular McDonald's
happened to be decorated with scenes from the Midwest. Looking
at a picture of a man standing in front of a barn in wheat country,
Mortensen suggested she could set the book on a farm in Kansas,
an idea which Smiley originally dismissed. The second incident was
a visit Smiley received from the actress Glenn Close who had read
and admired *The Age of Grief*. Struggling for conversation, Smiley
suggested the possibility of a production of *King Lear* told from the
oldest daughter's point-of-view, of course starring Glenn Close in
the meaty role of the Goneril character. Finally, about a year later,
on a drive to Minneapolis with her husband in winter, with everything dead and frozen, Smiley looked out the window and thought
again about her *King Lear* book and the potential Midwest setting.
Suddenly, the book began to form itself in her mind, Smiley remembers: "As had happened to me with each book, a sight of the
place where the novel was set caused the ideas and the characters
to jell, as if all at once. *A Thousand Acres* was now a presence. The
actual writing of it seemed more like a manageable detail than an
effort of creation" (Smiley, "Shakespeare," 1999, 169).

Yet, the book proved difficult to manage. Smiley relates that, of
all her books, *A Thousand Acres* was the hardest for her to write.
While she became swept up in *The Greenlanders* and describes her
work on that novel as exhilarating, writing *A Thousand Acres* took a
laborious and painstaking three years. Rather than speeding up

toward the end, her writing slowed down as she felt herself struggling more and more with Shakespeare through the course of the project. She imagined Shakespeare himself "wrestling with the original 'Leir' story [his source material for the play] and coming away a little dissatisfied, a little defeated, but hugely stimulated, just as [she] was." Smiley found the exhausting labor rewarding in the end. She writes:

I felt that I received a gift, an image of literary history . . . reflecting infinitely backward into the past and infinitely forward into the future. I knew that the wrestling I had done had not been only with Shakespeare, but also with his nameless predecessors, who carried forward this question of the nature of evil from the earliest human times. Since to me the greatest joy of writing and reading is connecting, this sense of connection through Shakespeare with the distant past has been the loveliest reward of writing *A Thousand Acres*. (Smiley, "Shakespeare," 1999, 173–74)

The book, of course, would make Smiley famous. Published in 1991, *A Thousand Acres* was awarded the Pulitzer Prize for fiction as well as the National Book Critics Circle Award. In 1997, the book was turned into a movie directed by Jocelyn Moorhouse and starring Jason Robards as Larry Cook, and Michelle Pfeiffer, Jessica Lange, and Jennifer Jason Leigh as Ginny, Rose, and Caroline Cook. Although the film received mixed reviews, it made Smiley's novel visible to an even wider audience.

After the success of *A Thousand Acres*, Smiley switched literary modes, next publishing in 1995 *Moo*, a big, comic novel which poked fun at the foibles of life at at a large land-grant university in the midwest, Moo U. While many readers suspected Moo U. was based on Iowa State University, where she had been teaching for fourteen years, Smiley firmly denies any explicit connections between the two schools, reminding readers that the book is a novel and Moo U. is a mythic, created world. The novel received fairly mixed reviews, most critics commenting on what they saw as Smiley's surprising switch from domestic tragedy to broad comedy while disagreeing about how funny the novel was and whether or not Smiley's satire was sufficiently scathing. Smiley herself explains her choice of the comic mode for *Moo*, when she discusses in an interview her desire to write a novel "in each of the four big genres: epic, tragedy, comedy, and romance" (Frumkes, 1999, 20). While *The Greenlanders* was her epic and *A Thousand Acres* her tragedy, *Moo* was Smiley's comedy.

Smiley finished her four genre project with the 1998 publication of her romance, *The All-True Travels and Adventures of Lidie Newton*. Set mostly in mid-1850's Kansas and Missouri, *Lidie Newton* tells the story of a "tall, plain woman" from Illinois who marries a Northern abolitionist, moves west, and confronts slavery in the territories. The novel was inspired, at least partly, by Smiley's rereading of two key nineteenth century American novels, *The Adventures of Huckleberry Finn* by Mark Twain, and Harriet Beecher Stowe's *Uncle Tom's Cabin*. Two years previously, in January of 1996, she had published "Say it Ain't So, Huck" in *Harper's Magazine*, a widely read article in which Smiley argued that, of the two novels, *Uncle Tom* treats slavery in a more complex, thoughtful way than *Huck Finn*, despite the praise heaped upon Twain's book and its unquestioned place in the canon of American literature. Smiley's article proved quite controversial, provoking an almost vitriolic response from both literary critics and the general reading public. Yet, Smiley says that both novels influenced *Lidie Newton*: "I like to see Huck as the dad and Harriet Beecher Stowe as the mom of my novel. . . . I don't like to kick dad or mom out of the house" (Frumkes, 1999, 20).

Smiley left her academic job at Iowa State the same year that the *Harper's* article appeared, moving with her husband and children to the Carmel Valley in California to live on a horse farm. Within a few months of their move, Smiley's husband, Stephen Mortensen, left her for another woman, prompting her third divorce and a hefty financial settlement paid by Smiley. Although the divorce necessitated a move to a smaller house, Smiley continued to buy horses, amassing at least nineteen at one time, including several thoroughbred racers and breeders. Her eighth full length novel, *Horse Heaven*, published in 2000, allowed Smiley to indulge her equine obsession as she explored the complex world of horse racing and betting. Another big book (570 pages) with a large cast, both human and animal, *Horse Heaven* was sometimes criticized for juggling too many characters and subplots, for being overly ambitious and ending up a jumble. Nevertheless, the majority of reviews reacted quite favorably to the novel, praising it as a witty, well-researched, and intricate delving into the minds of both horses and the people who live with them. Many readers also noted a new tone of optimism and a sense of redemption in *Horse Heaven*, a change from much of Smiley's earlier work.

At the age of fifty, Smiley seems to have made peace with the tangled, complex relationships of her past. She has found a new love interest since her split with Mortensen, but has no plans to remarry. "I come to the theory and practice of marriage at the start of the new millennium with a decidedly checkered past and an outsider's view," she muses. Always a close observer of family interaction, Smiley doesn't see the breakdown of the traditional family as "a dark and fearsome eventuality," but rather "as something interesting to observe, something that I have endured, survived, and actually benefited from, something that will certainly be part of the material from which my children build their lives" (Smiley, "Why," 2000, 151). This concern with the complexities of human relationships as they move through time is perhaps what unifies Smiley's seemingly disparate body of work. As Neil Nakadate observes, Smiley's fictive world is always concerned with cause and effect, with how choices people make affect their future; above all, it is a "moral fiction, a fiction of responsibilities, choices, costs to be paid, and messes to clean up" (23). Smiley herself concurs. In an interview with Bill Goldstein of the *New York Times*, she says, "That's the thing my work is always wrestling with: What do we make of the past? How do we get away from the past? How does the past hurt us? How do we find a way not to be tyrannized over by the past?" These are certainly the questions that Ginny Cook struggles with in *A Thousand Acres* as she confronts her traumatic past, a past which refuses to stay repressed.

2

The Novel

In A *Thousand Acres*, Jane Smiley transplants the tragedy of *King Lear* to the Cook family farm in Zebulon County, Iowa, in 1979. The Lear story is retold through the eyes of Lear's oldest daughter, Goneril, who, in the Shakespeare play, is one of two "unnatural hags" (II.4.274), the daughters who covet their father's kingdom and cast him out unmercifully for their own gain. Smiley, long dissatisfied "with an interpretation of *King Lear* that privileged the father's needs over the daughters'" (Berne, 1992, 236), sets out in the novel to understand and explain the motivations of the daughters which she felt were largely unexamined in the Shakespeare play. In doing so, she also writes, in the words of one reviewer, "a profoundly American novel" which explores how one family's hidden secrets are connected to patriarchal domination of both the landscape and of women.

This chapter begins with an overview of the novel that examines how it both parallels and departs from Shakespeare's *King Lear*. Next, it explores three major thematic threads which run through the novel (and which are closely entwined with one another): 1) appearance and reality—how appearances or surfaces may mask underlying truths; 2) ecological concerns—how greed and increasing technology may harm the land as well as how the land is intricately connected to the human body; and 3) feminist concerns—how the female body in particular is associated with the land and, like the land, may be dominated and controlled by men. Finally, the chapter will examine the ending of Smiley's novel, exploring how much hope she leaves us with after the multiple tragedies which befall the Cook family.

Overview/*King Lear* Parallels

BOOK I

Book I of A *Thousand Acres* introduces readers to life in Zebulon County, Iowa, as Virginia Cook Smith has always known it. The Cooks seem to lead a stable, fairly ordinary existence. The events Ginny describes seem the small, daily dramas of ordinary life and the people unremarkable. Yet, these initial chapters climax in two events which will set the rest of the novel into motion and lay bare the secrets which lie below the level of the visible: the return of Jess Clark to his father's house and Larry Cook's dividing up of his land among his daughters at Harold Clark's pig roast.

In these early chapters, Smiley establishes the novel's parallels to Shakespeare's *King Lear*. Shakespeare's play opens with the news that Lear will divide his kingdom among his daughters Goneril, Regan, and Cordelia. To determine what size share each will receive, Lear requests that each daughter declare the extent of her love for him. While Goneril and Regan play along, declaring their affection for their father in expansive terms, Cordelia says she loves her father as much as a daughter should and no more. Lear, enraged by her answer, cuts her out completely. Similarly, in Smiley's novel, Laurence Cook/Lear announces his plans to form a corporation and to give each of his daughters, Ginny/Goneril, Rose/Regan, and Caroline/Cordelia a share. When asked to affirm his decision, Ginny, despite an "inner clang," tries to sound agreeable and replies that Larry's plan "is a good idea." Rose, like Regan, tries to outdo Ginny in her claims of affection for her father and tells Larry that such a division of the land is a "great idea." Caroline, like Cordelia who refuses to participate in the love test, hesitates, replying that she doesn't know how she feels about the proposed corporation. Larry, like Lear, is angered by his youngest daughter's reluctance to play along, and quickly tells her: "You don't want it, my girl, you're out. It's as simple as that" (21). Book I closes by illustrating viscerally the rift between the two when Larry slams the farmhouse door in Caroline's face. The land transfer is sealed, though, as Ginny and Rose sign the necessary legal papers.

BOOK II

At first, these momentous changes in the Cook family seem full of promise. In Book II, we see the middle generation enjoying some of their new-found freedoms. Ty, Ginny's husband, begins to plan the enlarging of the hog operation, Rose's three month check up after her breast cancer surgery is positive. Perhaps most importantly, Jess Clark's presence adds a sociability and warmth missing from Ginny's life previously. He begins to come to supper and play monopoly with Ginny, Ty, Pete, and Rose. The *Lear* parallels continue as the Clark family comes to increasingly resemble the Gloucesters of Shakespeare's subplot. Harold Clark/Gloucester welcomes the prodigal son, Jess/Edmund, and begins to talk publicly about changing his will, which had previously favored the son who had stayed on the farm, Loren/Edgar. In Shakespeare's play, Gloucester allies himself with Edmund, his bastard son, at the expense of his true and loyal son, Edgar, promising the illegitimate Edmund at one point that he, rather than Edgar, will inherit Gloucester's land (II.1.82–84). Jess Clark also resembles Edmund in that both denounce conventional thinking on the part of their parents and neighbors which has harmed them. In a famous speech from the Shakespeare play, Edmund allies himself with "Nature" over the "plague of custom" which labels him a bastard and deems his brother Edgar to be Gloucester's only legitimate son. In the novel, Jess Clark confesses to Ginny his fury with his mother for never contacting him after he went to Vancouver to avoid being drafted: "What ideal did she sacrifice me to?" he angrily asks, "Patriotism? Keeping up appearances in the neighborhood?" (55). Jess is, at least metaphorically, the Clark's illegitimate son. Book II ends with Jess kissing Ginny, giving her a sensation she describes as strange: "a clumsy stumbling falling being caught," with the sunlight world narrowing to "a dark focus" (128). The kiss both scares Ginny and excites her with its promise of things to come.

BOOK III

The "stumbling" Ginny had mentioned at the end of Book II becomes apparent in Book III. Things start to go wrong; cracks begin to appear in the characters' surface happiness. Ginny remembers how some of the thousand acres were acquired by ethically murky means. Caroline, like Cordelia in *Lear*, marries Frank/France, but further splits the family by not inviting Rose or Ginny to her wedding. The monopoly games, a cause of such pleasure in Book II, sour. Larry wrecks his truck and must be picked up at the emergency room under suspicion of drunk driving. On the way

home, Ginny speaks harshly to her father for the first time. Just as
Goneril in the play tells her steward that Lear must be treated as a
child — "Old fools are babes again, and must be used/With checks,
as flatteries, when they are seen abused" (I.3.20–21) — Ginny feels
that she and her father have changed roles. "It was exhilarating,"
she muses, "talking to my father as if he were my child, more than
exhilarating to see him as my child. This laying down the law was
a marvelous way of talking" (148). Relations between Ty and Ginny
grow increasingly cold after this night. Ty admonishes Ginny for
not having more patience with Larry just as Albany in the play urges
Goneril to use caution in her treatment of Lear. When Ginny
becomes annoyed with Ty's calm demeanor, his "willful positive
thinking" (154), we may be reminded of Goneril's impatience with
Albany's "milky gentleness" and "harmful mildness" (I.4.338; 341).

But perhaps the central event of this section, and in many ways
the turning point of the whole novel, occurs when Ginny sleeps
with Jess Clark in the old pickup truck in the dump. Again, Smiley
takes her cue from *Lear*: Goneril offers to become Edmund's mis-
tress in the play. Following Ginny's betrayal of her marriage vows,
the pace of the novel speeds up dramatically. Larry, like Lear,
becomes increasingly unbalanced mentally, harshly castigates his
two older daughters, and wanders out into a violent storm. Smiley's
major departure from the Shakespeare play, of course, lies in the
fact that, unlike Goneril and Regan, Ginny and Rose are given
motivation for their antipathy toward their father. The shock of
Larry's words prompts Rose to tell Ginny the truth about Larry and
his late night visits to his daughters' rooms. While Ginny doesn't
remember the sexual abuse, she doesn't particularly object to Rose's
version of events. Book III culminates in the church potluck supper,
when Harold Clark publicly denounces Ginny and Rose as well as
his own son, Jess. There can no longer be any denying that all is
not well with the Cook and Clark families. The family's surface

prosperity and success have cracked wide open to reveal the shaky foundation beneath.

BOOK IV

Book IV details the unburying of many secrets. While Ty literally digs up the evidence from Ginny's fifth miscarriage, which she had kept from him, Ginny uncovers the memories of her past, specifically of her father's sexually abusing her. When she lies down in her old bed, the memories come flooding back and she must acknowledge that Rose was telling the truth. The Cook family's dispute over the division of the land is forced into the open when Ginny is served legal papers by her father's lawyer, Ken LaSalle. Ginny also reveals her true feelings to Jess Clark and is filled with shame when she realizes he doesn't return her love. Later, she acts uncharacteristically rude to Henry Dodge, her family's pastor, saying what she really thinks rather than what she is expected to. While Ginny is stripped of her illusions in this section and sees clearly for the first time in the novel, Harold Clark is blinded when he burns his eyes with chemicals from a clogged hose on his new tractor. This event parallels the blinding of Gloucester, Lear's neighbor and friend, in the Shakespeare play. Also, just as Cordelia and her father are reunited in *Lear*, at the end of Book IV, Ginny sees Caroline and Larry shopping together, apparently on quite friendly terms again.

BOOK V

The pace continues to escalate in Book V as the split between appearance and reality grows even greater. While their lawyer, Jean

Cartier, is able to portray the oldest Cook daughters and their husbands as proper, careful farmers, the family falls even further apart as tragedies and betrayals multiply. The death of Rose's husband, Pete, is told about in an offhand manner as is the fact that he had drained the water tank on Harold's tractor. Pete, then, is responsible for Harold's blinding just as Cornwallis, Pete's model in the play, causes the blinding of Gloucester, though Shakespeare's scene is much more bloody and violent (Cornwallis rips Gloucester's eyes out of his head). Smiley also retains the rift between the two oldest sisters which we see in *Lear*. While Goneril and Regan both fall in love with Edmund and fight over him, Rose in A *Thousand Acres* confesses to Ginny her own affair with Jess Clark. Seething with jealousy, Ginny decides to poison Rose, just as Goneril poisons her sister Regan in the play.

In her contemporary retelling of the story, Smiley casts the battle scenes at the end of *Lear* into the court battle which takes place near the end of A *Thousand Acres*. Just as Edmund's army, supported by Albany, Goneril, and Regan in the play, defeats Lear and Cordelia, the court case in the novel is decided in favor of Ginny, Ty, and Rose. Smiley's Caroline doesn't actually die as Cordelia does in the Shakespeare play; nevertheless, Larry, confused and senile, interrupts the court proceedings by shouting out that Caroline is dead. Larry, like Lear, dies soon afterward.

BOOK VI

While Shakespeare has both Goneril and Regan die at the end of the play—Regan is poisoned by Goneril and Goneril kills herself— Jane Smiley allows her narrator, Ginny, to survive. As critic James A. Schiff points out, a number of versions of the Lear story, both before and after Shakespeare, allow Cordelia and Lear to live, but

Smiley is the only writer that keeps the Goneril character alive at the end. Yet, in order to survive, Ginny must leave the farm, move to an anonymous apartment in the city, and reinvent her life as a single, working woman. While not the tragic ending of the Shakespearean drama, Smiley's ending is, at best, ambiguous. The Cook, Smith, and Lewis families have been destroyed, but perhaps at the end of the novel Ginny has a second chance at happiness.

Appearance and Reality

In the opening paragraph of the novel, Ginny carefully places the Cook family's thousand acres at the intersection of County Road 686 and Cabot Street Road in Zebulon County. Such a precise locating of the farm adds to the aura of traditional novelistic realism which Smiley establishes early on. It's the first of what will be a wealth of small, precise details about midwestern American farm life evident in Ginny's story. Her long explanation of where the farm is situated establishes Ginny as a careful observer of an orderly world which can be described and understood in an orderly fashion. This particular choice of opening also reveals the hierarchical nature of life in Zebulon County. Ginny's family and neighbors believe in placing things into their proper slot on a scale of prosperity and failure. The residents of this small piece of Iowa prairie share a provincialism and rootedness which Ginny associates with ancient cultures, isolated from the rest of the world and living life as it has always been lived. In fact, the world she has grown up in is so all-encompassing for Ginny that, as a child, she secretly believed the world really was flat and Zebulon County was the center of the universe. The emphasis here is on stability and rest rather than motion. Ginny imagines a seed, a rubber ball, or ballbearing com-

ing to rest in the perfect flatness of the land and sending down roots
into the soil.

Yet, such an opening also introduces the first disjunction between appearance and reality in the novel. While the book initially
seems to fit, in the words of critic Susan Strehle, the "genre of
domestic realism"—conventional in form and style and told by an
average, reliable, middle-American narrator—A *Thousand Acres*
gradually turns into something else altogether. Events become
larger and more terrifying than in the typical domestic novel; by the
end, characters attain nearly mythic status as their actions become
excessive, even monstrous at times. But the transition takes place
slowly. We get the first hint that Ginny might not be completely
satisfied with the life she describes when she confesses to her secret
pleasure in the car rides her family used to take. The car signifies
motion in a static world; the vastness of the farms which seem to
overwhelm Ginny are reduced to insignificance by the car's speed.
With the movement of the car, Ginny is able to indulge her own
secret longing for movement, for change, to assert herself against
the enormity of the world she finds herself in—a world in which
she is expected, as a child and a girl, to assume a subservient role
in the family hierarchy. Nevertheless, Ginny is able to repress these
hidden longings (as she will repress many other things in the course
of the novel) in favor of the comfort of her parents' world-view. She
concludes the opening chapter by asserting that "our farm and our
lives seemed secure and good" (5).

Appearances in this novel, though, are often deceiving. The
discrepancy between appearance and reality is—as one might expect from a writer whose purpose is to explore and fill out hidden
motivations in such a highly acclaimed literary work as Shakespeare's *King Lear*—one of the novel's main themes. In Chapter
Two, readers learn of many secret realities hiding behind the appearance of security and goodness outlined in the novel's opening

chapter. We find out about turmoil in the Clark family, that Jess, the oldest Clark son, had left the country when drafted for the Vietnam War and not been mentioned by the family again for thirteen years. Ginny tells us about Rose's breast cancer and her choice to send her daughters, Pammy and Linda, to boarding school against the family's wishes. We also find out about Ginny's first miscarriage and her jealousy of Rose's good fortune in carrying her own babies to term, that the sight of Pammy and Linda as infants affected Ginny "like a poison" for months.

Ginny's surface frankness and reliability as a narrator also begin to erode as the novel advances and she confesses her love for secrets. When Ginny continues to try and become pregnant after her third miscarriage, concealing the two later miscarriages from Ty, Rose tells her that she is "getting obsessed and crazy" (26). Ginny herself suggests to readers that she might not be exactly what she appears when she relishes one of the "benefits" of her "private project" to become pregnant: "it showed me a whole secret world, a way to have two lives, to be two selves. I felt larger and more various than I had in years, full of unknowns and also of untapped possibilities" (26). Ginny's outward self is so eager to conform to the environment she has been raised in, to be the good, obedient daughter and wife, that the only way she can imagine articulating her own wishes and desires is by displacing them onto a second, submerged self, kept carefully hidden from her family and neighbors. Ginny constantly negotiates between this outer, conforming self and her interior, more rebellious self. At one point she pictures herself confronting Larry about his trip to Des Moines to visit Caroline's office:

By the time I was frying the bacon and eggs and covertly watching him stare out the living-room window toward our south field, my plan to let him have it seemed like another silly thing. I couldn't find a voice to speak in, to say, "Were you down in Des Moines Thursday or not" or "Caroline thought you hung up on her when she called." This is something I do often, this phrasing and rephrasing of sentences in my mind, scaling back assertions and direct questions so that they do not offend, so that they can slip sideways into someone's consciousness without my having really asked them. (115)

Even in her own imagined scenario, Ginny is unable to "find a voice to speak in" because the questions she wishes to ask would contradict her carefully controlled public self. Always conscious of the appearance she is making, Ginny scales back, tries not to offend or to assert herself in any way.

Ginny's desire to appease, to appear dutiful, obedient, and accomodating is intrinsically connected to her position as the daughter of an Iowa farmer. "Most issues on a farm," Ginny informs us, "return to the issue of keeping up appearances" (199). She explains,

Farmers extrapolate quickly from the farm to the farmer. A farmer looks like himself, when he goes to the café, but he also looks like his farm, which everyone has passed on the way into town. What his farm looks like boils down to questions of character. Farmers are quick to cite the weather, their luck, the turning tides of prices and government regulations, but among themselves these excuses fall away. A good farmer (a savvy manager, someone with talent for animals and machines, a man willing to work all the time who's raised his children to work the same way) will have a good farm. A poor-looking farm diagrams the farmer's personal failures. Most farmers see farming as an unforgiving way of life, and they are themselves less than indulgent about weedy fields, dirty equipment, delinquent children, badly cared for animals, a farmhouse that looks like the barn. It may be different elsewhere in the country, but in Zebulon County, which was settled mostly by English, Germans, and Scandinavians, a good appearance was the source and the sign of all other good things. (199)

One sign of Larry's increasing mental confusion, then, is that he no longer abides by the farmer's code of keeping up appearances. After wandering into the storm, he calls both Marv Carson and Ken LaSalle in the middle of the night to complain of his daughters' treatment of him. Similarly, Harold Clark breaks with the absolute rule of appearance when he openly and explicitly denounces Jess along with Ginny and Rose at the church potluck supper. Ironically, as the Cook and Clark family quarrels become increasing public, Ginny and Rose—the characters most harmed by the community code that demands silence in order to uphold appearances—work harder than ever to keep up the illusion of family normality. As Ginny says, "The paramount value of looking right is not something you walk away from after a single night. After such a night as we had, in fact, it is something you embrace, the broken plank you are left with after the ship has gone down" (199–200). The two take pains to be seen in public, to speak to neighbors, to smile and joke and appear unconcerned about recent family troubles.

The oldest Cook daughters and their husbands cling even more firmly to appearances after they are served with legal papers by Caroline and Larry. Their lawyer, Jean Cartier, advises Rose and Ginny to "wear dresses every day, and keep the lawn mowed and the porch swept." He continues, "appearances are everything with a clause like this" (284). Cartier here is referring to the mismanagement or abuse clause in the original incorporation papers which stipulated that, under such conditions, the farm would revert to Larry Cook's ownership. Because neighbors will be called to testify in court as to the competence of the Smiths and Lewises, appearances in this case are indeed "everything": the neighbors' perception of how the farm is run will in fact determine the reality of who owns it. Ginny, so used to leading a double life, sinks thankfully into the routine that Jean Cartier has suggested: "I was so remarkably comfortable with the discipline of making a good appearance!" she says, "It was like going back to school or church after a long absence. It had ritual and measure" (285). Both Ginny and Rose respond to crises in their lives by cleaning obsessively. In the days before the trial, Ginny becomes the good wife with a vengeance, devoting herself mindlessly and excessively to her domestic duties. Similarly, following Pete's death, Rose insists that Ginny help her move the couch to vacuum beneath it, even though it's two o'clock in the morning. The sisters' obsession with cleaning in the novel betrays their early training in gender roles—women's work is done in the home. As Ginny tells us, "farm women are proud of the fact that they can keep the house looking as though the farm stays outside" (120). But, perhaps more significantly, Ginny's and Rose's constant cleaning suggests how dirty each feels as the victim of sexual abuse. Though largely unconscious, particularly on Ginny's part, the obsessive housecleaning represents the sisters' attempts to wash away and purify their own past experiences.

Despite their best efforts, however, and despite winning the court case, the neighbors do judge Ginny and Rose harshly. Harold Clark certainly feels that Larry's daughters have treated him unkindly, and most of the other neighbors echo his view. Toward the end of the novel, Rose rages about the fact that Larry is respected in the community: "Others of them like him and look up to him. He fits right in. . . . People pat him on the head and sympathize with him and say what bitches we are, and he believes them and that's that, the end of history" (302–303). In an interview, Smiley points out that she wanted the neighbors to act as almost a chorus, whose role in Greek tragedy is to comment on the action taking place. "In some ways," she explains, "the novel is a very somber game, but it's still a game. One of the parts of the game for me was presenting, through gossip and through what Ginny perceives, the normal interpretation of *King Lear* as a counterpoint to what we know is actually happening" (Berne 237). The normal interpretation of *Lear*, according to Smiley, is that Goneril and Regan are inherently, unmotivatedly evil in their treatment of their father. So the neighbors in A Thousand Acres, obsessed as they are with appearances, represent the typical interpretation of King Lear; they see Ginny and Rose as most readers of Lear see Goneril and Regan. But Smiley's point in the novel is to show the disjunction between appearance and reality; the neighbors' perception of the Cook family tragedy is, in fact, a misperception.

Ecology

THE LAND AND THE BODY

We have seen that Ginny's divided self, her determination to maintain an appearance of docile affability despite her inner turmoil, is closely linked to her upbringing on an Iowa farm where "appearance is everything." This connection between the individual and the land is, in many ways, the novel's dominant theme. A Thousand Acres begins with an epigraph from Meridel Le Sueur, a radical socialist writer and journalist popular in the 1930's, which reads in part: "The body repeats the landscape. They are the source of each other and create each other." Smiley illustrates Le Sueur's point when she entwines Ginny's family history — the past which lies below the visible present — with secrets of the landscape itself. When Ginny's paternal great-grandparents, Sam and Arabella Davis, first arrived on their newly purchased land in Iowa, they found half of it under standing water. Chapter Three of the novel details how the Davises, along with John Cook (who would later marry Edith Davis, Sam and Arabella's daughter, and become Ginny's paternal grandfather), lay tile lines undergound to drain the soggy fields. The tile drew water and warmed the soil, and contributed to the farm's prosperity. As a child, Ginny imagines the tile as a solid floor underground, a firm support which one could not sink beneath, like the checked tile floor in her elementary school bathroom. Yet, the adult Ginny acknowledges that the tile line has forged only a very fragile truce with nature. "The sea," she remarks, "is still beneath our feet and we walk on it" (16).

This image of water constantly flowing beneath the seemingly firm surface of the soil becomes a metaphor in the novel for the dark secrets which hide underneath the outwardly smooth operation of the family's day-to-day activities as well as for the passions which flow inside the characters' calm exteriors. When Ginny and Ty are preparing for bed the night after the disastrous Father's Day dinner, for instance, Ty suggests that Ginny and Rose could "handle" Larry better. Ginny replies that she doesn't understand her father, that there are "treacherous undercurrents" in their relationship at all times. "I think I'm standing on solid ground," she adds, "but then I discover there's something moving underneath it, shifting from place to place. There's always some mystery" (104). Outwardly friendly relationships among neighbors may conceal darker undercurrents as well. The Cook family profits from the failure of the Ericsons' farm, while Larry and John Cook's acquisition of land from Bob Stanley's cousin seems tainted by greed. Again, using the metaphor of the water underneath the land, Ginny muses that "the seemingly stationary fields are always flowing toward one farmer and away from another" (137). Family and community relationships, then, like the land itself, are not built on a solid foundation; they, too, are fragile and maintained only by hard work. And they hide secrets from the past.

As we have seen, Ginny's own feelings are often submerged and kept secret as well. One of her earliest memories as a child is squatting with Ruthie Ericson over the grate covering one of the farm drainage wells, dropping pebbles and sticks into the darkness below. Despite the fact that Larry has forbidden her to play at the grates, Ginny is drawn there, perhaps, she muses, by "the sound of water trickling in the blackness" (47). As an adult, these memories give her an "eerie feeling," no doubt because the grate represents an opening into the submerged undercurrents of family life she has worked so hard to repress. Ginny's attraction to hidden things emerges when she deceives Ty about the miscarriages. She not only leads Ty to believe that she has given up trying to become pregnant, but she also keeps her fourth and fifth miscarriages from him. Looking out at the familiar vista after supper one night and musing on her desire to have a child, Ginny recognizes that, while externally resigned, she had "wishes, too, secret, passionate wishes" (27). Indeed, we see the extent of Ginny's undercurrent of passion in the barely contained desire she feels for Jess Clark as well as in the exhilaration she experiences after talking to Larry as if to a child for the first time. Like the water under the soil of the farm, Ginny's powerful emotions and desires are hidden and contained by her compliant and docile demeanor. Yet, like the water under the land, her second self is still there, invisibly collecting harmful toxins which will erupt as poison later in the novel.

Smiley's correlation of the land with the human body gives the novel a richness and mythic resonance. Such a connection, Smiley explains in an interview, "goes as far back as the Bible. In Genesis, God makes people out of clay" (Winegar, 1992). Moreover, human fertility has long been linked in Western myth with the productivity of the land, while a diseased land has often been reflected in diseased human bodies. The medieval story of the Fisher King makes just such a connection. One of the main figures in medieval legends about the quest for the Holy Grail, the Fisher King was keeper of the Grail Relics. Yet, the King suffered a wound in both thighs, caused by the spear of Longinus, the same weapon that wounded Christ on the cross. These wounds, sometimes associated with the King's sinful nature, not only took away his virility, but caused his kingdom to become an infertile wasteland as well. Such myths, arising from ancient fertility cults and Celtic legend and Christianized in medieval chivalric stories, have been woven into the fabric of Western literature, from the thirteenth century writings of Robert de Borron to Tennyson's *Idylls of the King* to T. S. Eliot's great modern poem *The Waste Land* and up to today.

FARMING AND THE ENVIRONMENT

While, on the surface, the Cook family farm in *A Thousand Acres* is certainly not a wasteland, its seeming productivity masks long term problems. Again, appearances in this novel often hide dark, unpleasant realities underneath. When accepting the National Book Critics Circle Award for fiction in 1992, Smiley referred to some of the unpleasant truths which her novel exposes. She pointed out that *A Thousand Acres* presents a "complex argument against a certain kind of farming and land use that is leading us towards an environmental disaster, the destruction of the lives of people and of the moral life of our country" (Baker and Reid, 1992, 10). In a 1994 article published in *Sierra*, the magazine of the environmental activist group, the Sierra Club, Smiley clarifies her views on farming practices in the American Midwest. She begins by talking about the wealth and abundance of the Iowa prairies before European settlers arrived. In the novel, Ginny describes just such abundance:

For millenia, water lay over the land. Untold generations of water plants, birds, animals, insects, lived, shed bits of themselves, and died. I used to like to imagine how it all drifted down, lazily, in the warm, soupy water—leaves, seeds, feathers, scales, flesh, bones, petals, pollen—then mixed with the saturated soil below and became, itself, soil. I used to like to imagine the millions of birds darkening the sunset, settling the sloughs for a night,

or a breeding season . . . And the sloughs would be teeming with fish:
shiners, suckers, pumpkinseeds, sunfish, minnows, nothing special, but
millions or billions of them. I liked to imagine them because they were the
soil, and the soil was the treasure, thicker, richer, more alive with a past
and future abundance of life than any soil anywhere. (131 132)

Outwardly the very opposite of a wasteland, the soil is described by
Ginny as "land whose fertility surpassed hope" (131). In her *Sierra*
article, Smiley argues that, to the first Europeans, the Midwest
prairies seemed inexhaustible, both in their wide open spaces and
in their soil fertility. "The deepest topsoil," Smiley tells us, "was to
be found . . . in northeast Iowa, where it measured 20 to 25 inches."
    But, Smiley continues in her article, Europeans brought with
them heavy meat and dairy-based diets as well as farming practices
geared toward the regions they originally came from, regions which
were usually "mountainous, forested, stony, and cursed with poor
soil or unfavorable weather patterns." Europeans also brought with
them a hostility to diversity and to unfamiliar practices and beliefs.
They viewed nature as separate from and subordinate to men. They
"brought the habit of supporting large cities, which entailed an
emphasis on productivity as well as the continuous export of a
locality's best goods." These prairie settlers cleared away native veg-
etation, brought in the plow, and drained the land. While the initial
result was the amazingly fertile soil described by Smiley and imagined by Ginny in the preceding passage, nevertheless Smiley is
quick to point out that "the most important lesson of the flat fertile
lands is that appearances are deceiving."
    In her National Book Critics Circle Award speech as well as in
her *Sierra* article, Smiley criticizes the longterm effects of these
farming practices as environmentally devastating. Such effects include the erosion of the topsoil, a decline in the diversity of plant
and animal life, a depletion of some of the world's largest aquifers,

the chemical contamination of surface and underground water supplies, a rise of crop pests and diseases, and the general deterioration of rural life for the people who live there. Smiley argues that "the application of technology to agriculture on the North American prairies has not, so far, exempted our culture from the biological forces that have destroyed earlier civilizations. It is clear, rather, that big machines and strong chemicals have speeded them up."

Harold Clark's new $40,000 International Harvester tractor is the envy of all the neighboring farmers attending the pig roast, for whom larger land holdings and increased productivity seem to be constant goals. With this symbol, Smiley reverses a theme evident in Shakespeare's *King Lear*: the question of how much is enough. After both Goneril and Regan refuse to allow Lear to bring his hundred attendants if he should come to live with either of them, reasoning that he may as easily be served by their servants as his own, Lear responds: "O, reason not the need!" (II.4.259). He then goes on to argue that having more than we need is what separates men from the beasts. Smiley, on the other hand, seems sympathetic to the views of Goneril and Regan. In an interview, she details her fascination with excess, with going too far, with having too much. "I'm really interested in the idea of going too far," she says. "What happens in our lives that causes us to go too far, and what does it mean to go too far and get out of control and lose the things that somehow bind us socially, like good behavior? And then on the other end, how do you get back from so far away?" (Kidder, 1991). Larry Cook is clearly a man who goes too far in his assertion of ownership over his daughters. Linked to this is a capitalist excess criticized by Smiley in which increased productivity and gain become ends in and of themselves. Unlike Lear, she does not see the clear separation between men and the beasts as a good thing.

Larry Cook himself has not only struggled to expand the farm to its current thousand acres, but he has always been fascinated by new technologies. According to Ginny, he had a "lust for every new method designed to swell productivity" (45). When Larry sprayed for European corn borers in 1957, the Cook family farm was featured in an article in *Wallace's Farmer* entitled "Will the Farmer's Greatest Machine Soon Be the Airplane?". Ginny wryly notes her father's twin passions for more land and greater productivity when she remarks that the family might as well have had a catechism:

> What is a farmer?
> A farmer is a man who feeds the world.
> What is a farmer's first duty?
> To grow more food.
> What is a farmer's second duty?
> To buy more land. (45)

Indeed, when the family goes to church on Sundays, Ginny says it is to pay their respects, not to give thanks. The farm's fruitfulness is seen as the result of twenty-five years of constant labor, not as a gift of nature or of God. And just as the farmer's catechism replaces a church catechism, Larry Cook stands in for God. "Trying to understand my father," Ginny remembers, "had always felt something like going to church week after week and listening to the minister we had, Dr. Fremont, marshal the evidence for God's goodness, or omniscience, or whatever" (20). Ginny recalls that her father never seemed dwarfed by the landscape, that "the fields, the buildings, the white pine windbreak were as much [her] father as if he had grown them and shed them like a husk" (20).

The lust for more and more land in the novel is reflected in the monopoly games that Ginny, Ty, Pete, Rose, and Jess play in the evenings. The ultimate game of capitalism, Monopoly turns on collecting as much property as possible and improving that property as much as possible by building on it. The object is to bankrupt one's fellow players. As Anthony Quinn points out in his review of the novel, the Monopoly board is, for many readers, "our first and only taste of venture capitalism," (1992). It is also "a gloomy prefigurement of conflict about a real property, a real estate" in the novel. Just as the characters squabble over Monopoly real estate, a larger battle over the Cook family estate is brewing. The Monopoly building frenzy is reflected in the escalating plans for the farm's hog operation. Significantly, while the Monopoly games seem light hearted and fun in the beginning, they end badly, with Rose overturning the board and dumping the pieces into Pete's lap. Jess, at this point, astutely oberves that "unrestrained capitalism always ends in war" (140).

But the seemingly fertile and bounteous land, which the characters will fight over and work hard to improve, conceals dangerous toxins planted by the very same technological advances designed to improve on nature's productivity. Poisons and toxins become a recurring motif in the novel, used both to describe tainted relationships and the dangers of modern, chemically-enhanced farm practices. Early in the book, Ginny remembers that the sight of Pammy and Linda affected her "like a poison" after her first miscarriage. Poisons appear again when Marv Carson comes to breakfast at Larry's house and lectures Ginny about his strange eating regimen: "My main effort now is to be aware of toxins and try to shed them as regularly as possible." When Ginny asks which foods are toxic, Marv replies, "Oh, Ginny, goodness me, everything is toxic. That's the point. You can't avoid toxins" (29). While Marv's excesses seem silly, as the novel progresses, readers find that his beliefs are not so far-fetched as they might originally seem. When Ginny tells Jess about her five miscarriages, Jess is outraged that no one told Ginny what experts had known for at least ten years: that nitrates in the well water can cause miscarriages and death in infants. Smiley also hints that the high rate of death from cancer — both Mrs. Cook and

Mrs. Clark died of cancer and Rose battles breast cancer throughout the novel—might be linked to chemical run-off. In addition, Harold Clark's blindness is directly caused by the big machines and strong chemicals Smiley deplores in her *Sierra* article. He is sprayed in the eyes by anhydrous ammonia when he tries to unclog a hose on his $40,000 tractor.

Jess Clark, well aware of the poisons hidden underneath the seemingly fertile soil, offers an alternative to the highly technological and chemical farming practiced by Larry Cook and Harold Clark. Long interested in organic and smaller-scale farming, Jess, at the church potluck supper, excitedly tells Ginny about his visit to a farmer using alternative methods to work the land:

Ginny, I went to see that guy, the organic guy. I just got back. It was amazing. He hasn't used chemicals on his land since 1964. He's seventy-two years old and looks fifty. They've got dairy cattle and horses and chickens for eggs, but his wife only cooks vegetarian meals. They get great yields! Just with green manures and animal manure. The vegetable garden is like a museum of nonhybrid varieties. We had carrot bread and oatmeal from their own oats for breakfast, and carrot juice, too, and he had twenty different apple varieties in his orchard. I mean it was like meeting Buddha. They were so happy! (217)

Jess even describes this organic farm as a "paradise" which he desperately hopes Harold won't turn away from. Yet Harold and Larry and the vast majority of farmers in Zebulon County do turn away from Jess's vision of careful stewardship and paradise, turning to chemicals and technology to coax maximum production out of the land but poisoning it in the process.

While the myth of the Fisher-King and Eliot's *The Waste Land* imagine a physically or spiritually diseased human body infecting the landscape, Smiley depicts a diseased land poisoning the human body and turning it into an infertile wasteland. Infertility, in fact, is an obsession of the characters in *A Thousand Acres*. Ginny's life revolves around her attempts to maintain a healthy pregnancy. Caroline's late marriage, at the age of twenty eight, worries Larry, because he fears the union could be a barren one. As Rose tells Jess at the pig roast, "According to Daddy, it's almost too late to breed her. Ask him. He'll tell you all about sows and heifers and things drying up and empty chambers. It's a whole theoretical system" (10). While Rose, Ginny, and Jess can joke about Larry's views at this point, Ginny's worst perceptions of herself are voiced and made public when Larry castigates her after wandering away in the storm. Echoing Lear's curse upon Goneril in the Shakespeare play — "Into her womb convey sterility,/Dry up in her the organs of increase,/ And from her derogate body never spring/A babe to honour her" (I.4.275–278) — Larry calls Ginny a "barren whore" and a "dried-up whore bitch," linking her inability to bear children with what he perceives as her evil nature. Because Ginny cannot have children, she is, in Larry's view, an unnatural woman, useless as a sow who cannot be bred.

Feminism

ROLE OF FARM WOMEN

Larry Cook seems, then, to view his daughters as farm assets. And Ginny has been raised to accept this outlook as normal. In the novel's initial chapter, Ginny dutifully identifies the neighboring families, the Ericsons and the Clarks, according to the number of acres they own, their mortgage status, and the number of children in the family. We see that, in the world of Zebulon County, not just daughters but children in general are viewed as assets, as items owned by a family. In fact, Ginny admits that "acreage and financing were facts as basic as name and gender in Zebulon County" (4). When the Cook family adds a third child, Caroline, Ginny's father also buys a new car, indicating that the assets of the family have increased. While the Ericson and Clark families, with their two children each, continue to ride in farm pickup trucks, the Cook children ride in the luxury of a Buick sedan. "The car," according to Ginny, "was the exact measure of six hundred forty acres compared to three hundred or five hundred" (5).

Even Ginny's marriage is treated as an opportunity for the Cook family to increase their land holdings. Larry approves of Ty because the size of his farm, a hundred and sixty acres with no mortgage, is acceptable for the son of a second son. Also, Ty's father's death of a heart attack in the hog pen "was the ultimate expression of the right order of things" in Larry's view (12). While Ginny doesn't object to the marriage, she more or less seems to drift into it, not particularly aware of her own feelings, rather doing what is expected of her, trained into the habit of obedience to her overbearing father. When Ginny describes the less ambitious and more whimsical Ericsons, who much to Larry Cook's scorn take up the farming life for the pleasure they find in it, she especially remembers their animals— in particular, three trained dogs who "would perform a kind of drill, walking, lying down, sitting up, lying down again, and rolling over in unison on command" (44). The Ericsons' dogs, of course, parallel the Cooks' three trained daughters, who obediently perform at their father's command.

Smiley shows how women in the novel are not only subservient, but can become nearly invisible in the patriarchal world of Zebulon County. Ginny imagines her own point-of-view shrinking up and vanishing in the face of her father's opinions and pronouncements:

It was easy, sitting there and looking at him, to see it his way. What did we deserve, after all? There he stood, the living source of it all, of us all. I squirmed, remembering my ungrateful thoughts, the deliciousness I had felt putting him in his place. When he talked, he had this effect on me. Of course it was silly to talk about "my point of view." When my father asserted his point of view, mine vanished. Not even I could remember it. (176)

While Ginny's opinion dissolves in her father's presence, farm women in general have dissolved from history, overwhelmed by the stories of men. Ginny thinks about her own grandmother, Edith Davis Cook, who was married at sixteen to a man nearly twice her age. Edith's parents, Sam and Arabella Davis, almost seem to present John Cook with the gift of their daughter as a reward for his years of loyalty and hard work on the land. Reputed to be "a silent woman," Edith had children young, two of whom died in the flu epidemic of 1917, and died herself at the early age of forty-three. Ginny realizes that she knows nothing about what her grandmother Edith thought or felt, just that she lived her life surrounded by men, didn't drive a car, and probably had no money of her own. Marrying young and dying early is the norm for the women that Ginny knows — she herself marries at the age of nineteen, right out of high school. Rose, too, marries young and lives only to the age of thirty seven. Both Ginny's own mother and Jess Clark's mother die of cancer, leaving their husbands to live long lives as widowers. Neither John nor Larry Cook spends much time mourning the loss of his wife. Both make large land acquisitions immediately afterwards, their wives' deaths, as well as their lives, seemingly forgotten and never spoken about. It is only after Larry moves out of Ginny's childhood house that she has a chance to satisfy her curiosity about her mother's enigmatic existence. "Daddy's departure had opened up the possibility of finding my mother," Ginny muses (225). When women are valued only for the useful functions they fulfill, their deaths can render them invisible.

Part of Smiley's motivation for writing A *Thousand Acres* was to make the invisible visible, particularly the reasons why Goneril and Regan treat their father the way they do. When asked why she chose to retell such a canonical text as *King Lear*, Smiley responds, "I'd always felt the way Lear was presented to me was wrong. Without being able to articulate why, I thought Goneril and Regan got the short end of the stick." She continues, "There had to be some reason [Lear's] daughters were so angry. Shakespeare would attribute their anger to their evil natures, but I don't believe people in the Twentieth Century think evil exists without cause" (Schiff, 1998). Smiley is not the only reader to feel uncomfortable with the depiction of Goneril and Regan in *King Lear*. Tim Keppel, in his article "Goneril's Version: A *Thousand Acres* and *King Lear*," argues, following the lead of Shakespearean scholar Marianne Novy, that Lear's oldest daughters "are much less psychologically complex than most Shakespearean characters of comparable importance" (105–106). Koppel sees Shakespeare's depiction of the evil Goneril and Regan on the one hand set against the good Cordelia on the other as indicative of the way Western literature traditionally presents women "as devil or angel, Eve or Mary" (106). In her novel, Smiley tries to remedy this presentation of women. Her female characters are complex and layered, and like all humans, contain mixtures of both good and bad. While the women in Shakeseare's play have fixed identities—Cordelia remains good throughout and Goneril and Regan unquestionably evil—Smiley depicts women who are capable of change.

WOMEN AND NATURE

Just as Smiley insists on the complexity of her women characters, she also maintains that they should be valued for themselves, not according to their usefulness to men. When speaking with Martha Duffy of *Time* magazine, Smiley praises feminists who "insist that women have intrinsic value, just as environmentalists believe that nature has its own worth, independent of its use to man," (1991). Problems arise, she explains, when women are conflated with nature, when women, "just like nature or the land" are "seen as something to be used." In an interview with Suzanne Berne, Smiley argues that this is the view of women promoted by Shakespeare's *King Lear*:

Right before I started the novel, I felt a growing sense of a link between a habit of mind that perceives daughters and children as owned things. I felt, viscerally, that a habit of mind exists in our culture of seeing nature and women in much the same way. In fact, they represent one another in a lot of writing. That's a strong element of *King Lear*. Lear's always talking about nature and his daughters, conflating the two.

Smiley's point is that the connection between the land and the human body which the novel works so hard to explore, is, in Anglo-European cultures, especially pressing for the female body.

Such a conflation of women and nature is evident in American as well as British literature. In fact, such a correlation is one of the founding myths of America itself. Annette Kolodny, a feminist scholar of American literature who has examined metaphors used to describe the American landscape, argues that "America's oldest and most cherished fantasy" consists of "a harmony between man and nature based on an experience of the land as essentially feminine" (4). Such a connection stretches back to the earliest writings about America. Kolodny shows how the first European explorers and settlers described the new continent in feminine terms as a welcoming, maternal Paradise with, in the words of one early visitor, "all her Virgin Beauties" intact (4). Surely it's no accident that Jane

Smiley chose to name her main character Virginia Cook Smith. While Ginny's first name is the same as the name of the first territory settled by Europeans in the new world, her family and married names evoke early English explorers in the Americas. In fact, John Smith's relationship with the Indian woman Pocahontas was seen by many early Americans as a symbolic wedding between the native land and the Englishmen come to settle it. Critic Iska Alter points out that many of the character and place names in *A Thousand Acres*, including Ericson, Cabot, Drake, Lewis and Clark, LaSalle and Cartier, Stanley and Livingston, Amundson and Scott, Boone, Pike, Carson, and Crockett, link the novel specifically to "the early explorer/exploiters and settlers who first viewed, then described, and finally colonized the paradisal landscape of the New World" (1999, 155).

Ironically, Kolodny points out that the very process of colonization requires an ability to "master the land," to transform the virgin territories into something else — a farm, a village, a road. Smiley wants us to see that Virginia Cook Smith, like the Virginia Territories, is viewed by the men in her life, particularly her father, as something which must be controlled, domesticated. One of Larry's methods of mastery is to belittle the feminine. He can make Ginny overly conscious of her female body and ashamed of it as well. Soon after the relationship between father and daughter begins to sour, Ginny forgets to buy eggs for Larry's breakfast one morning. When she runs back to get some from her own house, she becomes very conscious of her body — "graceless and hurrying, unfit, panting, ridiculous in its very femininity." She adds, "It seemed like my father could just look out of his big front window and see me naked, chest heaving, breasts, thighs, and buttocks jiggling, dignity irretrievable" (114–115). In this passage, Ginny imagines her father's scorn for a disobedient daughter in terms of a female body which is out-of-control, untamed, ridiculous in its bounty of breasts, thighs, and buttocks. But to Larry, the female body is more than just ridiculous; it is foreign and even threatening — Ginny speculates that the Kotex box in the linen closet of Larry's home remained there so long because her father "never dared to touch it" (228).

It makes sense, then, that Larry's most insidious form of mastery over his daughters takes the form of incest. In dominating them sexually, he feels that he can control the very essence of what makes them female — their physical bodies. Just as he and his ancestors could transform the physical appearance of the water-logged virgin prairie into the cultivated and tamed one thousand acres, Larry Cook wishes to assert his dominance and control over his daughters' virgin bodies. As Rose tells Ginny: "We were just his, to do with as he pleased, like the pond or the houses or the hogs or the crops" (191). Smiley does not present the incest in the book so much as a matter of sexual desire as a desire for power, for possession. "In *A Thousand Acres*," Smiley observes when speaking to Martha Duffy, "men's dominance of women takes a violent turn, and incest becomes an undercurrent in the novel. The implication is that the impulse to incest concerns not so much sex as a will to power, an expression of another way the woman serves the man."

INCEST AND *KING LEAR*

Despite the response of some reviewers of the novel, such as Christopher Lehman-Haupt of *The New York Times*, that Smiley goes too far in making Larry/Lear a sexual abuser of his own daughters because it "robs" Lear of the "majesty" he possessed in Shakespeare's play, the incest theme is quite appropriate to a feminist retelling of the Lear story. Just as Smiley's purpose in the novel is to uncover some of the dark realities underlying comfortable appearances in Zebulon County, she also exposes possible hidden subcurrents in *King Lear* as well. Several articles published about the play in the 1980's, including those by Coppelia Kahn, Lynda Boose, and Mark Blechner, address the theme of incest in *Lear*. Boose, for instance, argues that Lear will not give Cordelia her portion of the kingdom unless she makes pledges of love to her father that would "nullify those required by the wedding ceremony" (333). Thus, in the opening scene of the play, Boose reads Lear's "darker purpose" as his attempt to prevent the upcoming marriage of Cordelia to either France or Burgundy, the suitors vying for her hand. Possessing incestuous desires for his own daughter, Lear can't bear the thought of her married to someone else.

In *A Thousand Acres*, Smiley hints at just such a reading. When Larry initially presents his idea that the family should incorporate and divide the farm, Ginny imagines that Caroline's hesitancy is complex: "Caroline would have said, if she'd dared, that she didn't want to live on the farm. . . . Caroline would have seen my father's plan as a trapdoor plunging her into a chute that would deposit her right back on the farm" (20–21). It's possible, then, to see Larry's sudden announcement of his desire to divide up the farm — a plan that surprises everyone listening and whose motivation remains mysterious — as his attempt to regain control over the one daughter who has been able to escape his grasp (and, apparently, his midnight visits as well). Caroline has been to college, works as a lawyer, and lives in Des Moines. Like Cordelia in the Shakespeare play, she is getting ready to marry. To Larry's apparent chagrin, she is marrying another Des Moines lawyer, Frank Rasmussen, a move which Larry might see as her determination to live in the city, away from the farm. Larry's decision to form a corporation, then, can be seen as an attempt to incorporate his youngest daughter back into the fold.

A subcurrent of incest in *Lear* may also be suggested in the love test which Lear forces upon his daughters in the opening scene. Readers of the play have long noted the improbability of such a test.

Most critics read the excessive responses of Goneril and Regan to the love test as self-motivated flattery. But it's a flattery that Lear himself certainly encourages and seems to expect. In requiring such responses from his daughters, might there not be the suggestion that Lear's relationship with his daughters is not an entirely natural and appropriate one? Cordelia's response to the love test in the play reinforces such a reading. She responds that she loves Lear "according to [her] bond, no more nor less" (I.1.93), emphasizing that Lear is asking her to proclaim a love beyond her filial bond. While Smiley may not go so far as to suggest that father/daughter incest literally occurs in *Lear*, her novel certainly points out the strangeness in Lear's relationships with his daughters and may lead readers to speculate further about the causes for conflict between them.

JESS CLARK

In *A Thousand Acres*, we see parent/child love overflow filial bonds not only with Larry Cook and his daughters, but in the Clark family as well. When Jess Clark tells Ginny in the dump that he's always been Harold's favorite son, he insists on describing the relationship as unnatural, as perverse: "The thing is, Harold loves me. He loves me like a lover" (127). Jess seems to be almost feminized here. Because he has not been the good son — in the patriarchal view of Zebulon County, he is labeled a coward and unmanly, for fleeing to Canada and avoiding service in Vietnam — he does not fit comfortably into the gender categories assigned by members of his community. Harold treats Jess like Larry treats his daughters, one minute seeming to "love" him excessively, in a sexualized way, the next humiliating him publicly like a jealous or betrayed lover.

As we've already seen, Jess's views on farming mark him as different from the other men in the novel. Alongside his alternative

vision of farming, and linked to it, lies Jess's appraisal of women.
Ginny recounts how Jess seemed to study her, to notice and observe
particulars about her, like her "nice ankles" which he admires. And
Rose appreciates the same qualities in him. She says, "He seems to
have this sense about my body . . . He just looks at it a lot, you
know, touches it as if he appreciates it. He says, you know, that my
shoulders are a nice shape, or that he likes my backbone. He sees
me differently than other men have" (300). Jess certainly sees her
differently than Pete does, who, after Rose's mastectomy, can no
longer bear to look at his wife's body. Smiley shows that an ability
to cherish the land, to nurture it rather than deplete it, is linked to
an ability to appreciate and care for individual human beings, especially women.

    Yet, readers might wonder, is Jess entirely what he seems? Al-
though, on the surface, he is quite different from any other men
Ginny or Rose know, he ends up betraying Ginny by sleeping with
her sister. While he appreciates Ginny's good qualities, he is unable
to return the love she feels for him. Rose initially defends Jess,
telling Ginny that she simply doesn't understand him. Ginny seems
to agree with this assessment, as she watches him in the courtroom
during the trial: "A stranger, he looked canny, almost calculating.
With no one looking at him and no occasion to exercise his charm,
his face was cool, without animation or warmth" (322). It is also
difficult to discern where Jess's loyalties lie. At the end of the novel,
Rose tells Ginny how Jess is late for dinner for one evening: "it
turned out he'd been to see Harold," Rose informs her, "and after
that it was just like watching your lover go back to his wife" (352).
Whether Rose's own ideas of fatherly love have been polluted by
her teenage experiences or whether the problem lies with the way
children in general are viewed in Zebulon County, Rose's statement
echoes Jess's earlier comment in the dump about the unnatural
relationship between himself and Harold. Finally, Jess seems to

betray even his environmental ideals when he gives up on the potential paradise of the organic farming operation he has established with Rose and returns to Seattle or Vancouver.

Readers are forewarned that a serpent might lurk in Jess's paradise. He is associated with snakes early in the novel, during his and Ginny's initial foray in the dump. While Jess appreciates the beauty of an area considered a wasteland by other characters, he also discovers a snake hiding under the heavily fragrant rosebushes. Jess is on easy terms with snakes, knowing the different species and even having a favorite. Ginny tells us, conversely, that Larry kills snakes, that he fears "untamed nature" (123). It's difficult to know exactly how to interpret this imagery. In the Genesis story of Eden, snakes are certainly associated with Satan, with evil and sin. Does Jess's familiarity with snakes suggest his ulimately flawed character? Or, on the other hand, might Jess's comfort with snakes simply suggest an open acknowledgment of the presence of sin and evil in the world, a refreshingly honest view when compared to Larry's attempts to deny and repress his own sinful actions? Or perhaps Smiley wants us to question the nature of evil itself. Is what the world calls evil necessarily so?

The snake imagery becomes even more complex when we see it applied to other characters besides Jess. Beginning with Ginny when she hears Larry's plans to divide the farm, characters are constantly licking their lips in snake-like gestures. Toward the end of the novel, Ginny imagines that Caroline's gaze "slithers" around the room. When Pete and Ginny talk at the quarry, a snake appears briefly and vanishes as the two walk back to their cars, possibly signaling the tragedy that will soon befall Pete there. The snake also suggests a ruined paradise; the blue sparkling water that Ginny remembers from her youth has been polluted and is choked with weeds and discarded junk. (Though just how Edenic the swimming hole really was during Ginny's childhood is open to question since she also remembers that she and her friends "pulled rusty objects out of the water with guileless curiosity" [247]). The snake imagery demonstrates Smiley's complex treatment of evil. In Shakespeare, there's no such ambiguity; Goneril, called a "gilded serpent" when she is ordered arrested (V.3.85), is unequivocally evil, though she tries to hide her true nature under a pleasing exterior. But everyone in *A Thousand Acres* seems to be hiding something, perhaps the land most of all, whose apparent bounty is the gilding over its polluted core.

So, how are we to view Jess? Is he too a gilded snake, pretending to be something he's not? Or does he genuinely challenge patriarchal ideas about the land and about women? Ginny's fascination with Jess arises from the fact that he's not like any other man she knows. In many ways, Jess embodies the rebellious side that Ginny has always supressed in her own character: "Everything he said about himself," Ginny tells us, "revealed the sort of life that I had always been afraid of" (51). Jess awakens Ginny to her own hidden self, causing her to recognize and acknowledge her dissatisfaction with her staid life and marriage. Yet, he also serves as the catalyst for Ginny's adultery, and, even more shocking, for her attempt to poison Rose. It's difficult to say whether Jess does Ginny more harm or good. Critic Iska Alter argues that, ultimately, Jess is not much different from the other men in Zebulon County:

Even Jess Clark, the novel's spokesperson for a fashionable environmentalism . . . sees land as an instrument upon which he can practice theory, just as he sees the bodies of women as sexual landscapes to test, to probe, to use. (1999, 156)

But perhaps this is too harsh a condemnation of Jess. His ideas about the environment are largely vindicated in the novel, and he seems to genuinely care for both Ginny and Rose, to value them in a way other men in the novel don't. In a book which is largely about perception and point-of-view, we see that the final view of Jess depends on who is looking at him, just as the final view of Goneril and Regan in the Shakespeare play depends on who is telling the story. While at the end Rose insists that Jess was "more self-centered and calculating" than Ginny believed he was, Ginny responds that "he was kinder and had more doubts" than Rose gave him credit for (351–352). Perhaps Rose's earlier explanation of Jess's character, that "he's just got more sides than most people we know" rings true in the end (303). Finally, Jess Clark remains an enigma, a complex character driven by complex motivations who disrupts the rigid gender expectations of his community and exposes poisonous secrets in doing so.

Ending

When Ginny walks out of her life in Zebulon County, she exchanges a world bound by the seasons and the passing of time for one that is man-made: an artificial and timeless world in which the air conditioner cools off the summer and the highway reduces the snow and rain of winter to mere scenery. Day fades imperceptibly into night as the lights in the restaurant, the parking lots, and the highways turn on and breakfast is served around the clock. Ginny also trades relatives and close neighbors for the impersonal world of customers, co-workers, and small talk. She remakes her life in the city to resemble as little as possible the farm life she has left behind. In fact, she admits that she considers this blur of urban routine her "afterlife," a life which doesn't contain a future: "Maybe another way of saying it," Ginny tells us, "is that I forgot I was still alive" (336).

Meanwhile, the afterlife of the Cook farm back in Zebulon County has also begun. The family farm which Ginny leaves behind is first divided, when Rose and Ty split the thousand acres down the road, then eventually lost altogether when it is sold to the ironically named Heartland Corporation. In a bit of poetic justice — Larry Cook's lust for increased technology and productivity will finally be carried out — Smiley depicts the passing of the era of small-scale family farming. The houses, vestiges of the humans that once farmed the land, are bulldozed or moved off the property to make way for the large corporate conglomerate that will take over.

DIFFERING CRITICAL VIEWS

While Smiley's ending certainly adopts a melancholy and lonely tone, readers of the novel have disagreed about how much hope the author finally leaves us. Critic James Schiff points out the ambiguity of the ending when he writes that "Ginny's decision to confront the past is nothing less than a victory, but one sees a mixed blessing in such a painful recovery." Other critics have agreed with Schiff that Ginny, though sad, is finally victorious. Jane Bakerman writes that, at the end of the novel, "Ginny is personally rather better off than before. She may not be happier, but she is certainly stronger and certainly more independent" (1992, 136). Most of the readers who think the end offers hope suggest that Ginny gains a voice and an understanding of the past. Iska Alter, for instance, argues that Ginny learns to see " 'without being afraid and without turning away' (355) that Eden is, and perhaps always has been, irreparably spoiled. Ginny's task, then, is to escape, to survive, and to tell the story" (1999, 156). And Mary Paniccia Carden (1999) adds, "While [Ginny] lacks traditionally defined rewards of femininity — she has

no money, no house, no man, no children of her own—she has
gained the alternate rewards of memory, knowledge, and voice."

Many critics see Ginny's gaining of a voice at the end of the
novel as rooted in her acknowledgment of the past. Neil Nakadate,
for instance, examines the scene in which Ginny's memories return.
She tells us, "I screamed in a way that I had never screamed before,
full out, throat-wrenching, unafraid-of-making-a-fuss-and-drawing-
attention-to-myself sorts of screams that I made myself concentrate
on, becoming all mouth, all tongue, all vibration" (229). According
to Nakadate, this scene signifies, for Ginny, "the beginning of
speech" (1999, 178). And perhaps this "beginning" comes to frui-
tion at the novel's close when Ginny seems to speak and behave
more forcefully than she ever has before. While Ginny's point of
view used to shrink away to nothing when confronted by her father
or husband, she is finally able to assert herself when Ty comes to
see her at the restaurant:

He opened his mouth to speak, but I stopped him with my hand. ". . . You
see this grand history, but I see blows. I see taking what you want because
you want it, then making something up that justifies what you did. I see
getting others to pay the price, then covering up and forgetting what the
price was." (342–343)

In addition, Ginny begins attending night school at the University
of Minnesota to study psychology. After several years of her lonely
restaurant life, she is again able to imagine a future for herself.
Finally, she receives custody of her beloved nieces, so is able to
reassemble for herself a new family life, even though Ginny tells us
that the girls "don't have a great deal of faith in [her] guardianship."
Nevertheless, they like Ginny and the three "get along smoothly"
(369).

Yet, even though Ginny's memories of sexual abuse have returned, the past still remains largely mysterious. When she confronts Caroline with the photographs from the wall of her parents' room, neither one can identify the enigmatic picture of a baby. Ginny explains the significance of this: "Everyone here is a stranger, even the baby. These are our ancestors, but they don't look familiar. Even Daddy doesn't look familiar. They might as well be anyone" (361). Remembering her father's actions does not seem to help Ginny know him or understand him any better. When Caroline responds that Daddy does look familiar to her, Ginny presses her about how familiar, and Caroline replies, "As familiar as a father should look, no more, no less" (362). Certainly an echo of the opening scene of *Lear*, in which Cordelia's response to the love test is: "I love your majesty/According to my bond, no more nor less" (I.1.92–93), the relationship between the sisters in the novel ends where the sisters' relationship in *Lear* begins. Smiley never allows Caroline and Ginny to reconcile, and Ginny never tells Caroline the truth about their father. Later, Ginny imagines Rose "pressing on [her] like a bad conscience" and concedes: "I should have told Caroline the truth" (364). If Ginny gains a voice by the end, this voice is still incomplete and imperfect.

Other critics read the ending as largely negative for different reasons. Barbara Mathieson, for instance, argues that while Ginny has achieved a certain amount of independence at the end of the novel, her relationship with the natural world — "the world of sensuously floating in a farm pond, of thrilling to the birds in the river's cut, the world of seasons" — is cut off completely, and that this constitutes a real tragedy. Mathieson adds that "nature is vanquished" on the Cook family farm as well:

Any hopeful signs in the novel's end for a renewed and meaningful life for Ginny and her nieces seem drastically undercut by the abandonment and waste of the natural world. . . . Ginny herself remains childless. And as for the quarry, the fertile waters, and the land itself, now firmly under the control of food conglomerates with no memory of lost fertility or former beauty, the outlook is grim indeed. (142)

Ginny actually concludes her story with the following lines:

And when I remember that world, I remember my dead young self, who left me something, too, which is her canning jar of poisoned sausage and the ability it confers, of remembering what you can't imagine. I can't say that I forgive my father, but now I can imagine what he probably chose never to remember—the goad of an unthinkable urge, pricking him, pressing him, wrapping him in an impenetrable fog of self that must have seemed, when he wandered around the house late at night after working and drinking, like the very darkness. This is the gleaming obsidian shard I safeguard above all the others. (370–371)

According to critic Marina Leslie, this passage "captures the difficulty of the incest survivor. Forgetting is a kind of death, but then so also is remembering" (1998, 48). While Leslie feels that readers can approve of Ginny's "ability to walk away," she also points out that we should not underestimate the emotional scars Ginny has received from her experiences. Finally, the "gleaming obsidian shard" that Ginny safeguards is not, according to Leslie, "forgiveness or a sense of her future," but rather "something hard and sharp and black that connects her to her past" (1998, 48).

LEAR AND THE ENDING

Perhaps another way that Smiley's ending rivals the tragedy of *King Lear*, despite the lower body count, is that so much remains unresolved at the end. One of the necessary elements of classical tragedy is that the tragic hero is supposed to recognize his own failings and feel remorse for them. In accepting personal responsibility for his own fall, the tragic hero gains self-knowledge and wisdom. Artistotle called this quality *anagnorisis*. Although Shakespeare's play doesn't condemn Lear's treatment of Goneril and Regan, Lear does recognize his failings as king and as father to Cordelia. When urged by Kent to enter a hovel during the raging storm, Lear shows a new gentleness and concern for others, urging Kent and the fool to go in before him. He laments:

> Poor naked wretches, wheresoe'er you are,
> That bide the pelting of this pitiless storm,
> How shall your houseless heads and unfed sides,
> Your looped and windowed raggedness, defend you
> From seasons such as these? O, I have ta'en
> Too little care of this! (III.4.28–33)

Having suffered himself, Lear realizes his own culpability in not caring more for the wretched inhabitants of his kingdom. Lear, at the end of the play, also begs forgiveness of Cordelia for the wrongs he has committed against her: "When thou dost ask me blessing I'll kneel down/And ask of thee forgiveness" (V.3.10–11).

While Lear recognizes his own shortcomings, Larry Cook never does. Rose's deep anger toward her father stems at least partly from his refusal to feel remorse. "There has to be remorse," she tells Ginny, "There has to be making amends to the ones you destroyed, otherwise the books are never balanced" (234). Rose's desire for retribution is tied to a longing for an orderly universe, for justice in the world: ". . . if there aren't some rules, then what is there? There's got to be something, order, rightness. Justice, for God's sake" (235). Rather than see Larry's increasing madness as divine retribution, Rose believes her father can take refuge in it: "Now there isn't even a chance that I'll look him in the eye, and see that he knows what he did and what it means. As long as he acts crazy, then he gets off scot-free" (235). What Rose longs for is the resolution of classical tragedy, the moment of *anagnorisis* that will lead to *catharsis*, or a purging of emotion. But Rose dies angry. And her legacy to Ginny is a lingering question: "Rose left me a riddle I haven't solved, of how we judge those who have hurt us when they have shown no remorse or even understanding" (370). The best Ginny can do, then, at the end of the novel, is to remember the darkness inside herself as she tried to poison Rose. This memory allows her to imagine and thus begin to understand the darkness that motivated her father's own "unthinkable urge." The "gleaming obsidian shard" she refers to in her final sentence is, finally, an acknowledgment of the evil in the world and inside of human beings. Ginny gains the self-knowledge and wisdom of the classic tragic hero that Larry never does.

3

The Novel's Reception

The press paid a great deal of attention to *A Thousand Acres* and gave the novel overwhelmingly positive reviews when it first came out in the fall of 1991. Reviewers especially liked Smiley's characterizations. Called "hauntingly real" by Gail Caldwell of *The Boston Globe* and "lively and thoroughly credible" by Nancy Wigston of *The Toronto Star*, the characters of *A Thousand Acres* seemed lifelike and interestingly complex to the novel's reviewers. In fact, Donna Rifkind of the *Washington Post Book World* wrote that the characters in the novel "overshadow the plot." Rifkind did not intend this comment as a criticism, but as a tribute to the "breathtaking" way Smiley managed to convey the characters' "shifting points of view." Particularly singled out for praise was Ginny, the novel's narrator. One of Smiley's "finest strokes," writes Ron Carlson in the *New York Times Book Review* is "the selection of her storyteller . . . It's Ginny's strange innocence that accompanies us through the novel and lends the story a marvelous and personal tension so credible it is chilling." Richard Eder of the *Los Angeles Times Book Review* adds that Ginny's voice is "supple and witty," compellingly evoking "the lives around her in all their tensions,

troubles, and pleasures." Julia Just of the *Wall Street Journal* felt
that the scenes between Ginny and her husband Ty were among
the strongest in the novel: "Ms. Smiley can describe compounding
strains in a marriage better than anybody, and the confrontations
between Ginny and Ty — quiet but devastating — are among the best
scenes in the book. She's superb at depicting the surface effects of
feelings 'too complicated . . . to name.'"

The reviewers also praised Smiley's rich depiction of the ordinary
minutiae of midwestern American life. Ron Carlson writes that "Ms.
Smiley's portrait of the American farm is so vivid and immediate —
the way farmers walk, what the corn looks like, the buzz of conversation at the community dinners — that it causes a kind of stunning
nostalgia." William Pritchard of *USA Today* agrees, pointing out
that Smiley has a "truly breathtaking intimacy with the detail of
family living" and that "her command of dailiness is masterly."
Diane Purkiss of the *Times Literary Supplement* points out that
"Smiley offers the detailed pleasures of the realist novel, un-
abashedly dwelling on the difficulty of vacuuming farmhouse car-
pets and on the business of growing tomatoes." Anthony Quinn of
The Independent (London) adds that Smiley assumes "the difficul-
ties of hog-farming and the best way to plant tomatoes will rivet our
attention, and she's right." This focus on the small, daily routines of
Midwestern farm life give the novel, in the opinion of Martha Duffy
of *Time*, an "exact and exhilarating sense of place, a sheer Americanness." Many of the reviewers, both American and British, made
similar comments. Gail Caldwell calls the book a "profoundly
American novel" while David Walton of *The Atlanta Journal and
Constitution* argues that the book, more than any novel he has read
in years, "lays fair claim to a subtitle that Ms. Smiley may not have
thought to, or was too modest to attach: An American Tragedy."
Anthony Quinn also refers to the novel as a "great American trag-

edy" while Claire Tham of *The Straits Times* (Singapore) calls it
"an American tragedy of mythic proportions."

While most reviewers approved Smiley's detailed and realistic
depiction of ordinary life, a few critics, mostly British, found the
amount of detail in the novel overwhelming. Frank Kermode of
The Guardian (London) pointed out that, while Henry James argued that specification in fiction is a good thing, in Smiley's novel,
"you are . . . told enough about the geology, the history, the evolving
agricultural technologies, the varied crops and the dollar cost of
these midwestern fields, to feel you've been given a more than
comfortable sufficiency" of the kind of specifics James called for.
And Diana Purkiss, while praising the novel's realistic pleasures,
also laments that "the novel is so reliant on these local pleasures
that it has little to offer in the way of the more cerebral entertain-
ment which admirers of minimalism have come to expect." But
perhaps most damning in this respect is James Wood's review which
appeared in the *London Review of Books*. Wood writes that, in *A
Thousand Acres*, "we learn far too much about hogs and slurry
systems and combine harvesters." He sees this extremely detailed,
specific style as "a very American kind of writing," arguing that it is
a style at least partly invented by creative writing programs and one
in which "detail is confused with storytelling." Finally, the accu-
mulated mass of detail "sinks" the novel for Wood.

Interestingly, many reviewers pointed out the "Americanness" of
the novel alongside their discussions of the *King Lear* parallels.
Almost every single published review of the book discussed the
novel's relation to *Lear* at least briefly, many writing that they had
at first been leery of Smiley's proposed revision of Shakespeare's
classic play. Gail Caldwell, for instance, writes that she "winced" at
the idea of Smiley's taking on *King Lear*: "It would be like going up
against Mozart, or Ted Williams: Half measures would be noble

but futile." Christopher Lehmann-Haupt of the *New York Times* observes that Smiley "has taken daring risks with her tragedy in a cornfield" and John Sutherland, writing for *The Seattle Times*, points out that "if the novel leans too much on the play, it might be useless on its own terms, and it might tell us nothing new." British reviewers, with perhaps even more invested in the sanctity of Shakespeare, their national literary treasure, were similarly skeptical about Smiley's proposed project. Anthony Quinn, in his review for *The Independent*, writes that "updating Shakespeare can be risky. How far can you go?"

Yet, despite these initial concerns, nearly all the reviewers agreed that Smiley carries off the Shakespeare parallels, largely because they saw the book as able to stand on its own merits. Caldwell writes that the real "litmus test of the novel" is whether it succeeds if we overlook the "thematic backdrop" of *King Lear*. And Caldwell, like most other reviewers, believes that it does. "*A Thousand Acres*," she writes, "is no half-measure. It is a full, commanding novel that manages to embrace *Lear* because its creator understands the ravages of Shakespeare's fallen king, yet she allows her own story to rely upon its own internal system." Ron Carlson agrees that *A Thousand Acres*, while invoking Shakespeare's play, doesn't "lean against *Lear* for support." He writes that "Jane Smiley takes the truths therein and lights them up her way, making the perils of family and property and being a daughter real and personal and new and honest and hurtful all over again." Martha Duffy argues that "it is a tribute to Jane Smiley's absorbing, well-plotted novel that it never reads like a gloss on Shakespeare." And David Walton concedes that, when summarized, "Jane Smiley's new novel sounds like a gimmick: a retelling of Shakespeare's *King Lear* story from the point of view of Goneril and Regan." Yet, Walton adds, "as in all Ms. Smiley's books, the surface action is merely a surface, beneath which a more complex, often contradictory story finds its way."

Most British reviewers, though not so unified as Americans in their praise, did feel that Smiley successfully carried off the Shakespeare parallels. Stephen Amidon, reviewing the novel for the *Financial Times* of London, writes that Smiley "has boldly adapted *King Lear* into a work that lives and breathes on its own merits." Anthony Quinn agrees, contending that Smiley's updating of the play "hit just the right balance, absorbing the structure of *Lear*, but allowing . . . all kinds of ambiguities and turnarounds." And like Gail Caldwell, Quinn points out that the book's triumph lies in the fact that it succeeds even if readers were to remain unaware of the *Lear* subtext: "In truth," Quinn argues, "the tragic momentum that *A Thousand Acres* gathers would in no way be diminished were the Shakespearean echoes to fall silent. It is an amazing novel on its own terms."

The one feature of the novel which the reviewers most disagreed about, and which sparked both heated criticism and praise, was Smiley's depiction of the family patriarch, Laurence Cook. Many reviewers admired Smiley's updating of the Lear figure; Julia Just of the *Wall Street Journal* and Nancy Wigston of *The Toronto Star* both nod to the "psychological truth" which underlies the conflict between Larry Cook and his daughters. Yet, several reviewers felt, along with Christopher Lehmann-Haupt of the *New York Times*, that "it seems too much to have made Larry Cook a sexual abuser of Ginny and Rose in their childhood." Lehmann-Haupt believes that Smiley's decision to present the Lear character in this way diminishes the lofty stature of Shakespeare's tragedy: "Lear himself is hugely egotistical," he writes, "but to push his selfishness into pathological monstrosity insults him retroactively and robs him of majesty." Other reviewers felt that Smiley's making Larry Cook a sexual predator made the novel less a work of art and too much a trendy piece of feminist social criticism. Richard Eder of the *Los Angeles Times Book Review* probably expresses this sentiment more fully than anyone else when he argues that the book, finally, is "a problem novel" and that problem novels simply don't work as art. While he writes that the "problem" in *A Thousand Acres* "is current and troubling," he also asserts that "fiction is not therapy." Eder believes the book is most successful when Ginny is denying her problems: "Before the Cook family secrets are vented and their disastrous consequences endured, [Ginny] is a person; afterwards, she is mainly a solution."

While Eder's review is thoughtful and balanced — he doesn't like the focus on sexual abuse, but he acknowledges the artistry of Smiley's writing and the subtlety of Ginny's voice in the first two-thirds of the novel — the most vitriolic responses to the book revolved around just this issue: incest. Notably, the most negative of the discussions of this topic did not appear until several years after the novel's initial publication, so that a backlash of a sort seemed to spring from the initial positive response the book received. In an article titled "They're Daddy's Little Girls," appearing in *Newsweek* magazine in 1994, Laura Shapiro attacks what she sees as the overuse of incest as a plot device in contemporary American fiction. She writes, "In just a few years, a ghastly trauma of childhood has been turned into an all-purpose literary ingredient, the Cool Whip of serious fiction. Editors and agents who track new fiction are encountering incest everywhere they look." She goes on to cite a magazine book-review editor who reports, "I'm not shocked by it, I'm bored. It's not a riveting plot device. There's something opportunistic about it." Shapiro cites another editor who claims that the common occurrence of the theme of incest is "all part of the culture of victimization we're in now . . . Somebody wants to jazz something up, they throw in a little incest." Significantly, Shapiro specif-

ically excludes Smiley from the harshest of her criticism, pointing
out that "not every incest story is a cliché plucked from daytime
TV." Yet, the general thrust of the article is to lump all recent books
dealing with incest together and to treat the authors of these books
as more interested in making money on the latest trend than in
writing works with lasting artistic merit.

This backlash against A *Thousand Acres* is even more evident in
Katie Roiphe's much-read 1995 article in *Harper's Magazine* called
"Making the Incest Scene." Like Shapiro, Roiphe argues that "incest has become our latest literary vogue" (65). But Roiphe does not
exclude A *Thousand Acres* from her contempt. In fact, she singles
Smiley out, devoting several paragraphs to attack the novel specifically. Roiphe writes that, in *A Thousand Acres*, "the ancient theme
of *Oedipus Rex* is accompanied by the clattering breakfast plates of
twentieth-century realism and the tragic, shimmering myth becomes an actual event described in pornographic detail" (65).
While one of Roiphe's main complaints about the overuse of incest
as a theme in contemporary literature is that it feeds readers' voy-
euristic appetites, one wonders how closely she has read Smiley's
novel; Larry Cook's attacks on his daughters are described in
anything *but* "pornographic detail." One suspects Roiphe makes
this accusation so that her criticism of A *Thousand Acres* will more
closely match the charges she levels against some of the other books
she discusses. But in Roiphe's view, Smiley is worse than the authors of certain "best-selling mass-market books" which address incest, because readers become especially frustrated "at the spectacle
of a skillful writer using such a cheap trick" (68). According to
Roiphe, "novels like Smiley's offer the perfect solution — the thera-
peutic thrill of delving into the past combined with the fast-food
convenience of pre-packaged interpretation: one overarching explanation for everything that's gone wrong. Such books operate on the
idea, borrowed from talk shows, that the complexity of human

character must be presented, analyzed, and solved in the space of one hour, not including commercials."

Roiphe's review of Smiley's novel is surely related to her own position as critic of the contemporary feminist movement. She first gained prominence after the publication of her 1993 book, *The Morning After: Sex, Fear, and Feminism* in which she lambastes the feminist movement, at least in its manifestation on U.S. college campuses, as overly concerned with issues of rape and female victimization. In fact, in her *Harper's* article, she argues that the early-90's crop of incest novels "comes straight out of a literary tradition that began in the Seventies with the profusion of men-are-bastards-fiction." So, a part of the later backlash against *A Thousand Acres* arises from its feminist content. Many later readers of the book, like Roiphe, saw the novel as "male-bashing" in its depiction of men, particularly in Smiley's decision to have Larry Cook commit incest. Novelist and essayist Charles Baxter, for instance, in his 1997 *Burning Down the House: Essays on Fiction* makes charges against *A Thousand Acres* which sound quite similar to Roiphe's. While Baxter argues that the novel first appears as if it will be about 1980s greed, and that such a story "would reveal clear if deplorable motives in its various characters," he adds, "But no: The book is about the essential criminality of furtive male desire" (8). With its revelation of incest, in a scene of recovered memory which could have come from *Geraldo*, according to Baxter, we see that many of the major characters are "doing their best to find someone to blame" (8). And like Roiphe, Baxter believes that one thing wrong not just with contemporary American fiction, but also with contemporary American culture, is that we celebrate victimhood. Tellingly, Baxter does not seem to have read the novel any more closely than Roiphe did, since he repeatedly mistakes Rose for Ginny and Ginny for Rose in his discussion.

Jack Fuller, writing in the *Chicago Tribune* shortly after the novel's publication, recognizes some of the issues which would arise in later criticisms of the book, but seems to have read the novel itself much more carefully than some of its later detractors. Fuller points out that, over and over again, the book "courts literary failure," yet that it "speaks with such growing authority that it overcomes all the dangers it creates for itself and triumphs even as its characters fall." One of the dangers that Smiley creates, according to Fuller, occurs when the truth about Larry Cook is revealed. At this point, Fuller feared that "This remarkably subtle and closely observed book was going to destroy itself in polemicism." Yet, he continues,

Smiley knows exactly what she is doing at every point, and her purpose is art rather than sexual politics. The ugliness of the truth about the father is important, but it is not what makes the book work. Its awful power comes from the way in which it examines the consequences of the truth it reveals. Its genius grows from its ruthless acceptance of the divided nature of every character, including its narrator.

While Fuller concedes that the novel "depicts men with as cold an eye" as any he has ever read, he also argues that the book is "too cunning" to be simply "an addition to the lengthening shelf of arguments against the human male . . . Its purpose is not to decide between the sexes but to examine the flaws in human nature that know no gender, from which the meanness and evil of men and women alike both spring." John Sutherland of *The Seattle Times* concurs with Fuller's reading, arguing that "there is a temptation to call this novel a feminist *Lear*, but it is more accurately a *Lear* for our democratic times. When Rose and Ginny stand up to their father, they are not standing up for their gender as much as they are standing up for their rights as individuals."

Despite the small but pointed backlash which arose in the later nineties, it's important to reiterate that the book was, on the whole, quite well received. The U.S. literary establishment generously rewarded the novel with various literary prizes, and reviewers compared it favorably to a number of books, both by Smiley and other writers. Julia Just and David Walton believe that, of all Smiley's work, A *Thousand Acres* most resembles the critically praised *The Greenlanders*, particularly in its precise descriptions of everyday life and its themes of family rivalry. Other reviewers argued that A *Thousand Acres* far outpaced anything Smiley had written previously. Ron Carlson pointed out that Smiley's earlier work had been praised by the literary world, but argued that "A *Thousand Acres* is the big book that will finally earn her the wider audience she deserves." Claire Tham of *The Straits Times* agreed, writing that, with this novel, Smiley "makes the triumphant leap from miniaturism to a broader, more epic canvas" and that the book is "a genuine tour-de-force." And Donna Rifkind of the *Washington Post Book World* adds that, while Smiley "has written beautifully about families in all of her seven preceding books . . . her latest effort is her best: a family portrait that is also a near-epic investigation into the broad landscape, the thousand dark acres, of the human heart."

The reviewers most clearly applaud Smiley's novel when they compare it to other highly respected literary works of the twentieth century. Theodore Dreiser's *An American Tragedy* was evoked in several reviews, though one critic argued that A *Thousand Acres* is even more like Arthur Miller's *Death of a Salesman* in its depiction of genuine despair. Gail Caldwell describes Smiley's writing as possessing a "quiet Chekhovian intensity," yet finally argues that the book "is a profoundly American novel" which is its greatest strength. For Caldwell, Smiley's depiction of the Cook family "begins to take on the wounded cast of Faulkner's damned" as family members become "dazed by the blows they've delivered as well as suffered."

Perhaps the reviewer most generous in his comparisons was Jack Fuller of the *Chicago Tribune* who describes *A Thousand Acres* as having the "prismatic quality of the greatest art." Fuller means that the novel seems to suggest different things when looked at from different angles, but that all "its contradictions are true." He goes on to discuss the universal themes evident in Akira Kurosawa's epic film *Ran*, also based loosely on the King Lear story, and in James Joyce's *Ulysses*, modeled on Homer's epic. Fuller concludes his review by arguing that what Jane Smiley "has made out of Shakespeare is strong enough to stand comparison with those magnificent, derivative works of art. This book very well may last."

4

The Novel's Performance

A Thousand Acres was a huge commercial and popular success. Several months after its initial publication in the fall of 1991, Smiley scored a major literary coup in the United States by winning both the National Book Critics' Circle Award for Fiction and the Pulitzer Prize. Following the announcement of these prestigious awards — the Critics' Circle on February 16, 1992 and the Pulitzer on April 7, 1992 — sales of the novel took off. According to Knopf, the novel's publisher, in the two weeks following the announcement of the Pulitzer they received orders for 10,000 copies, putting the novel into its sixth printing and bringing the total number of books in print on April 20, 1992, to 60,000. The novel also shot to the top of the *New York Times* Paperback Bestseller List, first appearing on April 26, 1992, and remaining on the list for thirty weeks. Being chosen as a Book-of-the-Month-Club Main Selection added to the book's popularity. Critically, the novel continued to gain attention as well. It received the *Chicago Tribune's* Heartland Award for fiction, and was nominated for the Irish Times-Aer Lingus International Fiction Prize.

But Smiley felt that her reputation as a writer was cemented when A *Thousand Acres* was banned from a public high school reading list in Lynden, Washington, in February of 1994. The novel was assigned to be read alongside *King Lear* in an Advanced Placement English class. Responding to complaints from members of a conservative Christian coalition called the Washington Alliance of Families, the school's principal removed the novel from the reading list, stating that it had "no literary value in our community right now" (Leslie, 1998, 33). The censorship was reported by newspapers across the country who quoted Smiley's response to the news: "Hot dog! I'm one of the big girls now," she said, adding, "I have wonderful, excellent, good company. All the best books have been censored." Yet, Smiley's initial reaction to the banning of her book soon turned to dismay when she discovered the reasons why:

When I first heard that my novel, A *Thousand Acres*, had been banned in Lynden, Wash., I thought, "At last!" My hard intellectual labors of linking Shakespeare with incest, Christianity, and ecologically destructive agriculture had finally been rewarded with what I've always thought they deserved—the outrage of the very people I had been intending to challenge and offend.

You can imagine my disappointment, then, when I discovered that the grounds for the banning was the same old, same old—use of the "f" word and heterosex between consenting adults (of course, there is also an inflammatory passage about a woman in bed looking under her sheet to contemplate her own body). (Leslie, 1998, 33)

Expecting objections to the novel for its criticism of patriarchy and capitalism, for its depiction of incest, or at least for its interpretation of Shakespeare, Smiley was disturbed that the novel's challengers didn't even seem to understand it. What she might not have known is that the parents who initially objected to the book didn't even have a child in the class and had read only small portions of the novel which were photocopied and passed around among students.

Although the novel fell off the *New York Times* Bestseller List at the end of April, 1993, it returned as a bestseller for six more weeks in the fall of 1997, when Jocelyn Moorhouse's film version came out. In preparation for the film, a new paperback edition of the novel was released, bringing the total number of copies in print to over two million by September 27, 1997. Moorhouse's film attracted a great deal of attention with its star-studded cast, particularly Jessica Lange as Ginny and Michelle Pfeiffer as Rose. Rounding out the cast were Jennifer Jason Leigh as Caroline, Jason Robards as Larry, Colin Firth as Jess Clark, and Keith Carradine as Ty. Lange and Pfeiffer had both worked hard to make the movie since 1992, when they both read early galleys of the book. Shooting finally began in Los Angeles and on location in Rochelle, Illinois in 1997. While the filming went smoothly enough, problems developed during the post-production period. Apparently, everyone on the set was disappointed with director Moorhouse's initial cut. The film's producers ended up hiring an outside editor to recut the movie, angering Moorhouse, who abruptly departed, threatening to remove her name from the film (Ansen, 1997, 82). Released on September 19, 1997, the final version of the film retained Moorhouse's name as director. Jessica Lange was nominated for a Golden Globe Award as best actress in a drama. (She was beaten by Judi Dench for her role as Queen Victoria in *Mrs. Brown*.) Yet, the film never made much of an impression at the box office and received mixed but mostly negative reviews.

Many of the reviewers condemned the movie for turning Shakespeare into melodrama, for being a "feminist tract" or "political propaganda" which tried to juggle too many current issues, or for presenting thin characters (particularly the men) who lacked motivation. Well known film critic Roger Ebert, among others, was particularly disdainful, writing that "A *Thousand Acres* is an ungainly, undigested assembly of 'women's issues,' milling about within a half-baked retread of *King Lear*. . . . the film substitutes prejudices for ideas, formula feminism for character studies, and a signposted plot for a well-told story." Reviewers who had actually read Smiley's novel tended to be kinder, often pointing out that the strengths of the book—its well-developed pace, nuanced family dynamics, and depiction of its characters' rich interior lives—were qualities hard to duplicate on screen. The one bright spot in the film mentioned by most reviewers was good acting by Pfeiffer and especially Lange. Even Roger Ebert called the two stars' performances "luminous." John Harti of film.com praised Pfeiffer for "heroically refus[ing] to glamorize her embittered character's rage" while Gary Kamiya of *Salon* wrote that "Pfeiffer only has to hit one note, but she hits it really well." Kamiya applauded Lange's performance in the film without reservation, arguing that "Jessica Lange captures Ginny's bewildered, sweet, resilient-yet-already-defeated personality in a wonderfully nuanced performance." John Harti agreed, adding that, although Lange "can't save" the film, "she comes close."

While the film is a fairly faithful adaptation of the novel, it does omit several of the novel's important themes, most tellingly the relationship between the poisoned land and the poisoned human body. The only indication we get of dangerous farm practices is Jess's very brief reference to run-off in the well water when Ginny explains why she doesn't have children. This scene contains the only mention of Ginny's five miscarriages. Marv Carson never alludes to toxins, neither Rose's cancer nor the cancers that killed Mrs. Cook and Mrs. Clark are linked to dangerous chemicals, Harold Clark's blinding by anhydrous ammonia is completely omitted, and, surprisingly, so is Ginny's attempt to poison Rose. The relationship between the sisters, then, is cleaned up and made a bit less ambiguous, as is the character of Jess Clark. In the film, Jess proves to be unequivocally bad: he leaves Rose when she gets sick again, while in the book Jess is gone long before Rose's cancer returns. The movie also downplays Jess's interest in organic farming and leaves out the reasons for his initial departure from Zebulon County—the fact that he was fleeing the Vietnam War. So perhaps some of the film reviewers' complaints about unclear motivations and thin characters are justified. Larry Cook's conduct in the film is also less motivated than it is in the book. The slow-developing first third of the novel is covered very quickly in the film, so that we see little of Larry's rigid, controlling, and increasingly odd behavior leading up to the climactic scene in the storm. A film certainly cannot cover as much ground as a novel, but Moorhouse perhaps omitted too much in her desire to focus so fully on the relationship between the two oldest Cook sisters and their status as incest survivors.

Even so, many of the negative reviews of the movie seemed motivated by the same kind of backlash against feminism evident in later discussions of the book by cultural critics such as Laura Shapiro, Katie Roiphe, and Charles Baxter. Several of the film reviewers objected to the focus of the film itself rather than to how well or how artistically the film carried out its objectives. And their political agenda seems to have prejudiced their judgment. While Roiphe appeared to have read a different book when she says Smiley depicts the incest in "pornographic detail," Roger Ebert seems to have watched a different film when he says that Rose describes her father's visits in the middle of the night in "lurid detail." The subject matter is so distasteful to these critics that they see what they expect to see rather than what actually happens. It is perhaps easy to dismiss *A Thousand Acres*, both the novel and the film version, as too trendy or politically correct, particularly in a decade which does seem to glorify family dysfunction and perversion via talk shows and other popular culture mediums. Recent questions about the legitimacy of "repressed memory syndrome" have also fueled a certain amount of critical disdain for both the book and film. Sparked by implausible tales of Satanic cults, rapes of children as young as six months old, and other unlikely scenarios, skeptics have understandably begun to question the scientific underpinnings of such a syndrome. Yet, to dismiss a work of art out of hand for touching on topical or politically sensitive matters seems short-sighted at best. Smiley, in an interview, comments that all of her novels "have an underlying political purpose." But she adds that "the aesthetic ideas and the interactions of the characters and the movement of the language always overwhelm whatever I originally thought my message was" (Ross, 1990 413). Thoughtful critics will continue to evaluate Smiley's novel for how intelligently and artistically she conveys her political purpose, rather than condemning her for her choice of subject matter. General readers around the world clearly have embraced the novel. By 2001, it had been translated into nineteen foreign languages: German, Italian, French, Portuguese, Spanish, Danish, Finnish, Swedish, Japanese, Korean, Chinese, Hebrew, Greek, Turkish, Latvian, Slovene, Croatian, Bulgarian, and Czech. A *Thousand Acres* continues to sell well, remains a favorite with reading groups and book clubs, and is appearing more and more frequently on college syllabi.

5

Further Reading and Discussion Questions

OTHER WORKS BY SMILEY

Ranging from family drama (*Barn Blind, At Paradise Gate, The Age of Grief, Ordinary Love* and *Goodwill*), to mystery (*Duplicate Keys*), to a fourteenth century epic (*The Greenlanders*), to comedy (*Moo, Horse Heaven*), to historical romance (*The All-True Travels and Adventures of Lidie Newton*), Jane Smiley's published fiction is quite diverse. Readers who enjoyed *A Thousand Acres*, though, might best appreciate four of the books leading up to her Pulitzer Prize-winning bestseller. Like *A Thousand Acres, At Paradise Gate* (1981) depicts the relationship between a father and his three very different daughters. It, too, provides a close examination of family dynamics as the daughters gather to say good-bye to their dying father. Though somewhat uneven, the short story collection *The Age of Grief* (1987) shines in places. The best story in the collection is the title novella, which is told by husband, father, and professional dentist David Hurst who tries desperately to hold his family together despite his wife's having fallen in love with another man. As in A Thousand Acres, Smiley beautifully renders the nuances of married life from the point of view of a character who does not fully understand his own emotions and desires. Ordinary Love and Goodwill (1989), two novellas published together, continues to explore the pressures that can cause families to self-destruct. The first novella, "Ordinary Love," is told by a fifty-two-year-old divorced mother of five, whose affair with a neighbor twenty years previously had torn apart her marriage. "Good Will" is narrated by a father, a Vietnam veteran whose obsession with living self-sufficiently damages his family.

The Smiley novel that really ranks as a masterpiece able to sit alongside of A Thousand Acres is her 1988 epic The Greenlanders. The novel can be a bit difficult to get into, but it's well worth the effort. Perhaps the most profound accomplishment of this novel is Smiley's ability to create a whole world contained within the covers of the book—a world rich in a wealth of detail about the ordinary, daily lives of people in a culture long since past. A fascinating read, The Greenlanders follows the lives of a large group of characters from several different generations, again exploring complex and subtle relationships between family members and among neighbors.

WORKS BY OTHER AUTHORS

If you liked A Thousand Acres, you might consider reading some of the following works by other authors which resemble Smiley's novel either in subject matter, theme, or style:

Anne Tyler — especially Dinner at the Homesick Restaurant (1982), The Accidental Tourist (1985), and Ladder of Years (1995)
  Tyler's novels, like Smiley's, often focus on family dynamics. Tyler is especially good at showing ordinary but often lonely or out-

of-place characters who have experienced tragedy or failed relationships in the past. These characters often survive by creating new,
nontraditional family groups for themselves. *Dinner at the Homesick
Restaurant* explores the troubled Tull family from the perspectives
of mother Pearl and each of her three children in turn. *The Accidental Tourist*, made into a film in 1988, tells the story of travel
writer Macon Leary, damaged emotionally since the accidental
death of his son and divorce from his wife. Macon's staid and
cautious life changes drastically when he meets a flamboyant dog
trainer. In *Ladder of Years*, forty year old Delia Grinstead walks
away from her home and family to create a new life and identity for
herself.

Barbara Kingsolver—especially *The Bean Trees* (1988), *Animal
Dreams* (1990), and *The Poisonwood Bible* (1998)

Kingsolver, like Smiley, does not shy away from political activism
in her novels. She, too, writes about feminist and environmental
concerns. While her characters might be more quirky than Smiley's,
Kingsolver nevertheless manages to make them intensely real and
sympathetic. Her first novel, *The Bean Trees*, follows the journey
west of Taylor Greer, a bright, irreverent young woman trying to
escape rural, poverty-stricken Kentucky where she grew up. Along
the way, Taylor takes in a three year old Native American girl with
whom she eventually forges a very close tie. *Animal Dreams* depicts
the life of Codi Nolinas, a young woman who leaves a medical
residency to return home to Arizona to care for her aging father and
teach high school biology. Part of the story is told through the letters
written home by Codi's younger sister Hallie who is working as an
agricultural development aide in Nicaragua. Like *A Thousand Acres*,
the novel explores a close relationship between two sisters and their
father as it also critiques environmental abuses. *The Poisonwood
Bible* is told by the wife and four daughters of evangelical Baptist

Preacher Nathan Price who, in 1959, moves his family to the Belgian Congo in Africa for missionary work.

Jane Hamilton—A Map of the World (1994)

A *Map of the World* focuses on the lives of Alice and Howard Goodwin who have moved from the city to a dairy farm in Wisconsin where they live with their two young daughters. When a neighbor's child drowns under Alice's care, her world starts to fall apart. Things get even worse when Alice is accused of sexually abusing a child at the school where she works as a part time nurse. Her family descends into a nightmare of guilt and accusations as seemingly trivial lapses in attention or judgment change Alice's life forever. Jane Hamilton's novel resembles *A Thousand Acres* not because each touches on the subject of child sexual abuse, but because both authors so skillfully present the psychological complexity and rich interior lives of their troubled protagonists.

Dorothy Allison— Bastard out of Carolina (1992)

A finalist for the National Book Award, Allison's novel tells the story of Ruth Anne Boatwright, known as Bone, a young girl raised in poverty in the 1950s in Greenville, South Carolina. When her waitress mother marries Daddy Glen, Bone gains a stepfather who beats and sexually abuses her. The novel is both funny and painful as Bone relates her experiences in a wonderfully idiosyncratic and South Carolina-inflected prose style. Like Smiley, Allison creates a world that is utterly believable in its precision of detail and moving in the beauty of its style.

Bobbie Ann Mason —especially Shiloh and Other Stories (1982) and *In Country* (1985)

Set mostly in rural and small town Kentucky, Mason's work, like *A Thousand Acres*, focuses on ordinary, plain people doing the best they can to sort out and muddle through changing and often difficult family relationships. Sometimes described as "K-Mart Realism," Mason's work, like Smiley's novel, provides detailed descriptions of contemporary rural American life. *Shiloh*, winner of the PEN/ Hemingway Award for fiction and a finalist for the National Book Critics Circle Award, is a quietly ironic collection of stories about sometimes bewildered characters coping with the encroachment of urban America along with the changing vistas of their personal relationships. *In Country* is a coming-of-age story about 17 year old Samantha Hughes whose father died in the Vietnam War before she was born. When her mother moves to Lexington, Sam stays behind in small town Hopewell, Kentucky, to live with her uncle Emmett, also a Vietnam veteran. The novel details Sam's attempts to learn more about the war that killed her father and scarred her uncle.

Joyce Carol Oates — Foxfire (1993)

Though very different in tone and style from A *Thousand Acres*, Oates' *Foxfire* can also be read as a feminist novel and thus might appeal to fans of Smiley's book. Set in upstate New York in the 1950s, *Foxfire* profiles the activities of a working class girl's gang. Most of the gang girls come from troubled families and find in the gang the closeness and kinship they're missing in their biological families. Like A *Thousand Acres*, Oates' novel explores close bonds between women as well as social forces which oppress women. Though not actual sisters like Ginny, Rose, and Caroline, the girls in *Foxfire* become "blood sisters" through the gang's initiation ritual.

WEBSITES

There is not yet an official Jane Smiley website or electronic discussion forum, but quite a bit of information about Smiley and her work is available on the web. Perhaps the most useful website for someone wanting to learn more about Smiley is:

The *New York Times* online site:
http://www.nytimes.com/books/00/04/02/specials/smiley.html

This site provides, among other things, *New York Times* reviews of all Smiley's books, including Ron Carlson's "King Lear in Zebulon County"; a response to Smiley's provocative *Harper's Magazine* article, "Say it Ain't So, Huck"; and an interview focusing mostly on *Lidie Newton*. If you've never visited the *New York Times* on the web before, the site requires you to register. But registration is free, must be done only once, and is well worth it for the wealth of information available.

Several on-line interviews with Smiley were conducted as publicity for *Lidie Newton* and *Horse Heaven*, her two most recent novels, and focus primarily on those books. These include:

Atlantic Unbound interview from May 28, 1998
http://www.theatlantic.com/unbound/bookauth/ba980528.html
BookPage interview from April 2000
http://www.bookpage.com/0004bp/jane smiley.html
BookPage interview from April 1998
http://www.bookpage.com/9804bp/jane smiley.html
Random House page on Jane Smiley
http://www.randomhouse.com/features/smiley

A good interview which touches on several of her novels and which covers more general topics, including the process of writing and research, how Smiley's writing has developed over the years, and her literary influences is:

> *Fiction Writer* interview with Anne Bowling, January, 1999
> *http://www.writersdigest.com/newsletter/smiley2.html*

For a short analysis of *A Thousand Acres* which first appeared in the journal *Notes on Contemporary Literature*, see:

> Scott Holstad Essay
> *http://www.well.com/user/sch/smiley.html*

An excellent website for those who would like to learn more about Jocelyn Moorhouse's film version of the novel is available at:

> The Internet Movie Database
> *http>//www.imdb.com/*

This address will take you to the main page for the database. Then you can simply search for *A Thousand Acres* using the dialogue box provided. The database contains comprehensive information about the film, including a still photo gallery, video clips, full cast and crew listings, reviews, awards received, memorable quotes, box office performance, and more.

DISCUSSION QUESTIONS

The following discussion questions will help you explore your own ideas about the book more fully. They may be especially useful to guide book club or reading group discussions of the novel.

1. Consider the novel's epigraph from Meridel Le Sueur. How does this quote shape and inform the book?

2. Is Ginny an entirely reliable narrator? Can we completely trust her perception of events? Why do you think Smiley chose Ginny to narrate the story? How would the book have been different with a different narrator?

3. What is the significance of the fact that the land used to be completely under water and that it was painstakingly drained by tile lines laid by hand? How does the image of submerged undercurrents permeate the novel?

4. What motivates Caroline's uncertainty about the incorporation and division of the farm in the beginning? Is it simply concern for her father or is it more complex?

5. How did Mrs. Cook's early death affect the family? What might be different had she lived?

6. Some reviewers argued that Smiley went too far in making Larry Cook sexually abuse his own daughters—that such a decision robs the Lear character of his majesty, making him unambiguously bad. Do you agree or disagree with this assessment?

7. Do you consider Ty a villain or a victim in the novel? What are his strengths? What are his failings?

8. How has the past shaped Rose's personality? How do Rose's reactions to her abusive childhood differ from Ginny's? Which sister's response (if either) seems a healthier one to you? Do you sympathize more with one sister than with the other? Why?

9. Reviewers disagreed about the success of the last third of the novel, some arguing that it spins out of control, others that it is riveting. Julia Just of the *Wall Street Journal*, for instance, writes that "the unending string of disasters . . . seems more than

strictly necessary, while the characters' motivations sometimes hover on the outer edges of plausibility." Yet, Nancy Wigston of the *Toronto Star* argues that, throughout the novel, "Smiley's characters are lively and thoroughly credible . . . her plot tense and explosive." How did you react as events in the novel escalated, as disaster seemed to pile upon disaster, as the pace became increasingly frantic? Did you find some incidents hard to believe? Did your interest pick up or diminish as the novel progressed?

10. What are we supposed to think about Jess Clark? Are his ideas about organic farming sound? What about his treatment of Ginny? Why do you think he returns to Vancouver or Seattle at the end, abandoning Rose and his dreams of enlightened farming?

11. Why does Ginny never tell Caroline the truth about their father? Is it weakness of character? Or does she act out of kindness? Should she have told?

12. How do you read the ending of the novel? Is it entirely tragic? Does Smiley leave us with any hope for the future?

FOR FURTHER READING

Articles and Books by Jane Smiley

"Afterword: Gen-Narration." *Family: American Writers Remember Their Own*, eds., Sharon Sloan Fiffer and Steve Fiffer. New York: Pantheon Books, 1996. 241–47.

The Age of Grief. New York: Alfred A. Knopf, 1987.

The All-True Travels and Adventures of Lidie Newton. New York: Alfred A. Knopf, 1998.

At Paradise Gate. New York: Simon and Schuster, 1981.

Barn Blind. New York: Harper and Row, 1980.

Duplicate Keys. New York: Alfred A. Knopf, 1984.

The Greenlanders. New York: Alfred A. Knopf, 1988.

Horse Heaven. New York: Alfred A. Knopf, 2000.

"Imposing Values." *New York Times Magazine*, 20 Sept. 1992: 28–29.

Moo. New York: Alfred A. Knopf, 1995.

Ordinary Love and Good Will. New York: Alfred A. Knopf, 1989.

"Shakespeare in Iceland." *Transforming Shakespeare: Contemporary Women's Re-Visions in Literature and Performance*, ed. Marianne Novy. New York: St. Martin's Press, 1999. 159–79.

"So Shall We Reap." *Sierra* 79, March/April 1994: 74+.

"Why Marriage." *Harper's Magazine*, June 2000: 151.

Interviews and Background Information about Jane Smiley

Baker, John F. and Calvin Reid. "17th NBCC Awards: Idealism Meets Commercialism." *Publishers Weekly*, 23 March 1992: 10.

Berne, Suzanne. "*Belles Lettres* Interview." *Belles Lettres* 7, Summer 1992: 36–38. Reprinted in *Contemporary Literary Criticism* 76 (Yearbook 1992), ed. James P. Draper. Detroit: Gale Research, 1993. 229–238.

Goldstein, Bill. "Every Time You're Free, You're Lonely. A Talk with Jane Smiley." *New York Times on the Web*, 4 April 1998, 1 March 2001. <http://www.nytimes.com/books/98/04/05/specials/smiley-interview.html>.

Kidder, Gayle. "Smiley Pushes People Over the Edge; Author Creates Characters Who Lose Control." *San Diego Union Tribune*, 21 Dec. 1991: E1.

Lewis Burke Frumkes, "A Conversation with Jane Smiley". *The Writer*, May 1999: 20.

Nakadate, Neil. *Understanding Jane Smiley*. Columbia, SC: U of S. Carolina Press, 1999.

Ross, Jean W. "[Smiley, Jane (Graves) 1949–] CA Interview." *Contemporary Authors* New Revision Series 30, ed. James G. Lesniak. Detroit: Gale Research, 1990. 411–13.

Winegar, Karin. "In Her Book, Earth, Women Are Victims of Mistreatment." *Star Tribune* [Minneapolis], 9 April 1992: E1+.

Critical Essays on *A Thousand Acres*

Alter, Iska. "*King Lear* and *A Thousand Acres*: Gender, Genre, and the Revisionary Impulse." *Transforming Shakespeare: Contemporary Women's Re-Visions in Literature and Performance.* Ed. Marianne Novy. New York: St. Martin's Press, 1999. 145–158.

Bakerman, Jane S. " 'The Gleaming Obsidian Shard': Jane Smiley's *A Thousand Acres*." *Midamerica: The Yearbook of the Society for the Study of Midwestern Literature.* East Lansing, MI: Midwestern Press, 1992. 127–137.

Carden, Mary Paniccia. "Remembering/Engendering the Heartland: Sexed Language, Embodied Space, and America's Foundational Fictions in Jane Smiley's *A Thousand Acres*." *Frontiers: A Journal of Women Studies* 18.2, 1997: 181–202.

Leslie, Marina. "Incest, Incorporation, and *King Lear* in Jane Smiley's *A Thousand Acres*." *College English* 60.1, January 1998: 31–50.

Mathieson, Barbara. "The Polluted Quarry: Nature and Body in *A Thousand Acres*." *Transforming Shakespeare: Contemporary Women's Re-Visions in Literature and Performance.* Ed. Marianne Novy. New York: St. Martin's Press, 1999. 127–144.

Schiff, James A. "Contemporary Retellings: *A Thousand Acres* as the latest *Lear*." *Critique: Studies in Contemporary Fiction* 39.4, Summer 1998: 367–81.

Strehle, Susan. "The Daughter's Subversion in Jane Smiley's *A Thousand Acres*." *Critique: Studies in Contemporary Fiction* 41.3, Spring 2000: 211–226.

Other Relevant Critical Sources

Baxter, Charles. *Burning Down the House: Essays on Fiction.* St. Paul, MN: Graywolf Press, 1998.

Blechner, Mark J. "Lear, Leir, and Incest." *American Imago* 45, Fall 1988: 309–325.

Boose, Linda. "The Family in Shakespeare Studies." *Renaissance Quarterly* 40, 1987: 713–742.

Kahn, Coppelia. "The Absent Mother in *King Lear*." *Rewriting the Modern Europe*. Ed. Margaret W. Ferguson. Chicago: U of Chicago Press, 1986: 33–49.

Kolodny, Annette. *The Lay of the Land: Metaphor as Experience and History in American Life and Letters*. Chapel Hill: U of North Carolina Press, 1984.

Novy, Marianne L. "Patriarchy, Mutuality, and Forgiveness in *King Lear*." *Love's Argument: Gender Relations in Shakespeare*. Chapel Hill: U of North Carolina Press, 1984: 150–163.

Roiphe, Katie. "Making the Incest Scene: In Novel After Novel, Writers Grope for Dark Secrets." *Harper's Magazine* 291, Nov. 1995: 65+.

Shapiro, Laura. "They're Daddy's Little Girls." *Newsweek* 24, Jan. 1994: 66.

Reviews of A Thousand Acres

Amidon, Stephen. "Shades of Lear — Stephen Amidon on a Novel Unafraid to be Derivative." *Financial Times* [London], 17 Oct. 1992: Books 20.

Caldwell, Gail. "King Lear in the Cornfields." *The Boston Globe Books*, 3 Nov. 1991: 91.

Carlson, Ron. "King Lear in Zebulon County." *New York Times Book Review*, 3 Nov. 1991: 12.

Duffy, Martha. "The Case for Goneril and Regan." *Time* 138, 11 Nov. 1991: 92–94.

Eder, Richard. "Sharper Than a Serpent's Tooth." *Los Angeles Times Book Review* 10, Nov. 1991: 3+.

Fuller, Jack. "King Lear in the Middle West." *Chicago Tribune Books*, 3 Nov.1991: 1+.

Just, Julia. "Lear in Iowa: Family Farm, Family Trouble." *Wall Street Journal*, 13 Nov. 1991: A14.

Kermode, Frank. "What Maisie Was Anxious to Know." *The Guardian* [London] 13 Oct. 1992: Features 11.

Lehmann-Haupt, Christopher. "On an Iowa Farm, a Tragedy with Echoes of Lear." *New York Times*, 31 Oct. 1991: C20.

Pritchard, William. "Evocative Bounty of A *Thousand Acres*." *USA Today*, 1 Nov.1991, final ed.: 5D.

Purkiss, Diane. "Uncovering Iowa." *Times Literary Supplement*, 30 Oct. 1992: 20.

Quinn, Anthony. "The Terrors of the Earth." *The Independent* [London] *Weekend Books Page*, 17 Oct. 1992: 26.

Rifkind, Donna. "A Man Had Three Daughters. . . ." *Washington Post Book World*, 27 Oct. 1991: 1+.

Sutherland, John. "*Lear* for Our Democratic Times—Novel Parallels Shakespeare, But Story Stands on Its Own." *The Seattle Times*, 24 Nov. 1991: K11.

Tham, Claire. "Lear with a Twist." *The Straits Times* [Singapore], 20 March 1993: Life; Books 14.

Walton, David. "A *Thousand Acres*." *The Atlanta Journal and Constitution*, 24 Nov. 1991: N10.

Wigston, Nancy. "*King Lear* Rewritten for Our Times." *The Toronto Star*, 7 March 1992: J18.

Wood, James. "The Glamour of Glamour." *London Review of Books*, 19 Dec. 1992: 17–18.

Reviews of the film version of A *Thousand Acres*

Ansen, David. "A *Thousand Acres* (movie reviews)." *Newsweek*, 22 Sept. 1997: 82.

Ebert, Roger. "Lear Lite: Epic Redux Falls Short by *Acres*." *Chicago Sun-Times*, 19 Sept. 1997, late sports final ed.: Weekend Plus 38.

Harti, John. "And Nowhere To Go." *Film.com* 1997, 6 June 2000. <http://www.film.com/film-review/1997/9546/109/default-review.html>.

Kamiya, Gary. "Old Molester Had a Farm." *Salon.com*, 19 Sept. 1997, 6 June 2000. <http://www.salon.com/sept97/entertainment/acres970919. html>

Schickel, Richard. "A *Thousand Acres* (movie reviews)." *Time*, 22 Sept. 1997: 93.

Reviews of Other Smiley Works

Bernays, Anne. "Toward More Perfect Unions." Rev. of *The Age of Grief*. *New York Times Book Review*, 6 Sept. 1987: 12

Humphreys, Josephine. "Perfect Family Self-Destructs," Rev. of *Ordinary Love and Goodwill*. *New York Times Book Review*, 5 Nov. 5 1989: 1, 45.

Kakutani, Michiko. "Books of the Times." Rev. of *The Age of Grief*. *New York Times*, 26 August 26, 1987: C21.

Untitled Rev. of *At Paradise Gate*. *Kirkus Reviews* 49, 1 August 1981: 963.